"A must-have, must-read, must-share book. Dr. Tim Witmer, a seasoned soul-physician, calmly enters his consulting room. It is full of anxious people. Many have been dosing themselves on narcotic or toxic prescriptions or self-cures but continue to experience personal and relational meltdown. His diagnosis is superbly clear; his prescription is powerful. His prognosis is honest. Even his instructions are a pleasure to read. Plus, his medicine works. Try *Mindscape*—a great book!"

Sinclair B. Ferguson, Author; Professor of Systematic Theology, Redeemer Theological Seminary, Dallas, TX

"Our culture breeds anxiety, anger, and escapism. 'Anxious about our relationships we are alone together.' To counter this multi-headed hydra, Tim Witmer gives us a tour of the truly beautiful mind, the biblical mind, that returns us to the sanity of 'my Father's world.'"

Paul E. Miller, Director of seeJesus; author of *A Praying Life* and *A Loving Life*

"As colleagues, Tim Witmer and I probably spend a fair amount of time worrying about the same things. ' thus a pleasure to see that he has spent considera reflecting on this problem from a biblical a perspective. This book is both a work of Tim dismantles the myths we tell a of construction, as he focuses th great biblical truths that give and perspective on, our place is a straightforward pastoral book, w a very real need in the anxious times in wi. .ve."

Carl R. Trueman, Paul Woolley F. .essor of Church History, Westminster Theological Seminary, Philadelphia

"I worry. In fact, I worry a lot. Tim Witmer's biblical and practical book is refreshing for someone like me. He reminds me of the truth and of the rest, joy, and life at the center of the truth. I'll probably still worry, but I'm going to be a lot better because of this book and you will be too. Read it and be glad!"

Steve Brown, Key Life radio broadcaster; professor (emeritus), Reformed Theological Seminary, Orlando

"Our culture thinks about human problems by focusing on the pathological extremes: panic attacks, anxiety disorders, and the like. But *Mindscape*, like Scripture, starts at the other end of the spectrum. It focuses on those normal 'pathologies' that beset all of us who ever feel worried, fearful, or apprehensive. This book is full of good sense because it is full of God and his ways. Wherever *you* land on the anxiety spectrum, take *Mindscape* to heart. You will become a wiser human being, guaranteed!"

David Powlison, Executive Director, CCEF; author

"Do you ever worry? If so, this book is for you. In an age of self-help manuals, theology-lite, and moralistic preaching, *Mindscape* is truly refreshing. Indeed, if carefully read and inwardly digested, it is life-changing. Tim Witmer proclaims a fully sovereign, yet truly comforting God who intervenes in the midst of very real affliction from without and persistent sin from within. He brings the simplicity and depth of the seasoned pastor to the reader. And the gospel of grace is on every page."

William Edgar, Professor of Apologetics and Boyer Chair in Evangelism and Culture, Westminster Theological Seminary, Philadelphia

"We worriers often see ourselves as victims of the unseen future's threatening possibilities. With pastoral wisdom and grace-grounded transparency, Tim Witmer summons us to resist anxiety proactively. Paul's famous directive to replace worry with thankful prayer (Philippians 4:6–7) is just the beginning of God's agenda to free us from our fears (4:8–9). Christ's Spirit can refurnish our 'mindscape,' replacing preoccupation with what might go wrong with concentration on the Savior, who makes all things gloriously right."

Dennis E. Johnson, PhD, Professor of Practical Theology, Westminster Seminary, California; author of *Him We Proclaim*; coauthor of *Counsel from the Cross*

"To be human is to worry. It's something we all do. You can't avoid it. With that in mind, Tim Witmer introduces you to Paul while he is in jail in Philippi. Each chapter rivets the reader's anxious mind on better things to think about. If you find yourself overwhelmed and filled with worry, read Tim's book. It will give you some wonderful things to think about as well as a gracious Savior to talk to in the midst of it all."

Dr. Timothy S. Lane, President, Institute for Pastoral Care; coauthor of *How People Change*

"*Mindscape* is a helpful guidebook for any of us who have ever thought wrongly about the issues of life. With pastoral warmth, Dr. Witmer shows us how we can change the way we think and apply the gospel. *Mindscape* shows us that a new way of thinking can lead to a new way of living."

Scott Thomas, Associate National Director, C2C Network; coauthor of *Gospel Coach*

Mindscape

WHAT TO THINK ABOUT
INSTEAD OF WORRYING

Timothy Z. Witmer

New
Growth
Press

WWW.NEWGROWTHPRESS.COM

New Growth Press, Greensboro, NC 27404
www.newgrowthpress.com

Cover Design: Faceout Books, faceoutstudio.com
Interior Typesetting & eBook: Lisa Parnell, lparnell.com

ISBN 978-1-939946-71-3 (Print)
ISBN 978-1-939946-77-5 (eBook)

Library of Congress Cataloging-in-Publication Data
Witmer, Timothy Z., 1953–
  Mindscape : what to think about instead of worrying / Timothy Z.
Witmer.
    pages cm
  Includes bibliographical references.
  ISBN 978-1-939946-71-3 (pbk.) — ISBN 978-1-939946-77-5
(ebook) 1. Thought and thinking—Religious aspects—Christianity.
2. Worry—Religious aspects—Christianity. I. Title.
  BV4598.4.W58 2014
  248.4—dc23
                                                    2014020476
Printed in the United States of America

21 20 19 18 17 16 15 14   2 3 4 5 6

To my wife Barbara—

who in my mindscape is an oasis
in the desert of life, who brings me joy
every time I think of her.

Contents

Acknowledgments

I would be remiss if I didn't include some important expressions of appreciation. I am thankful for the officers and congregation of Crossroads Community Church (PCA) who heard much of this material in a sermon series several years ago. My appreciation also goes out to Barbara Juliani at New Growth Press for seeing the value in this book and helping to sharpen its focus. Last but not least, my deep love and appreciation to my wife Barbara, to our children Sara and her husband Joel, Rebecca, Nathan, and grandchildren Mikayla, Katie, Emma, and Ben, who sometimes make me worry, but who always bring me joy.

1

What Were You Thinking?

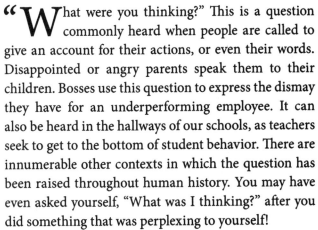

"What were you thinking?" This is a question commonly heard when people are called to give an account for their actions, or even their words. Disappointed or angry parents speak them to their children. Bosses use this question to express the dismay they have for an underperforming employee. It can also be heard in the hallways of our schools, as teachers seek to get to the bottom of student behavior. There are innumerable other contexts in which the question has been raised throughout human history. You may have even asked yourself, "What was I thinking?" after you did something that was perplexing to yourself!

No matter what context it's used in, the question points to the fact that we are rational creatures made in the image of God. Human behavior doesn't just come out of nowhere but is the result of a thoughtful process.

The same truth is revealed when a crime is committed. One of the first questions asked is, "What was the motive?" This is just another way of saying, "What was he thinking? What was the reasoning behind the perpetrator's actions?" This question was one of the first asked in the wake of the wave of mass killings in recent years. It is expected that even criminals will have "thought through" the reasons for their deeds, regardless of how warped those reasons might be.

Having worked closely with people for over thirty years as a pastor, I have become convinced of the importance of addressing the ways in which we think about the challenges of life. If you would allow us to take a look at the features that define the landscape of your mind—your "mindscape," as it were—what would we see? What are the thoughts that occupy your mind throughout the day and perhaps into the night? Are you a worrywart? Are you always imagining the worst possible scenario that can happen in any situation? When you think about the future is your mind filled with fear? How do you deal with your day-to-day anxieties? Probably, like most of us, you do worry—about specific situations and things that haven't even happened yet.

If you had access to the mindscape of another person for twenty-four hours, you would probably be shocked at what you saw. Think about it: How many of *us* would like someone else to have twenty-four hours of access to *our* thought lives? I wouldn't.

This is particularly alarming as you consider the words of Proverbs 23:7 (NASB): "For as he thinks within himself, so he is." Our thoughts give us a picture into what we are really like, and this can be very discouraging. If the mind is the "window of the soul," our mindscape can betray an inner darkness that casts a shadow over our thoughts, words, and deeds. But our condition is not hopeless—and this is the point of the pages that follow.

This book is not designed to be an academic tome on cognitive or behavioral theory; rather, it is a practical guide for real people with real problems. It is written for everyone who has ever worried about anything!

And, it is written from a biblical perspective. Although composed long ago, the Bible is not irrelevant to our current worries, struggles, and desires. In every age and every culture God's Word provides everything we need for life and godliness (2 Peter 1:3). The Bible is God's "user's guide" for all the equipment he has given us, including our minds. If you don't share my beliefs about the Bible, *please don't put this book aside* or immediately dismiss what you find on these pages. I'm guessing that you have already looked for answers elsewhere, but your mindscape is still cluttered with the same old scenery. Perhaps this is a good time for you to consider what the Bible says about the challenges that you face. I honestly believe that if you wrestle with the concepts introduced on these pages, new vistas will open in your own mindscape. You will experience a new way of thinking and, therefore, a new way of living—where you will gradually see your worries and fears replaced by a growing trust in God's care for you.

Most of the Bible passages we will consider together come from a man who had the world on his shoulders. He had undertaken a monumental enterprise and had experienced opposition at every turn. Many who had previously been his enthusiastic supporters were now his avowed enemies. The opposition he experienced was not merely in the form of hateful words and behind-the-back scheming. His opponents tried to "snuff him out" on several occasions and had at least gotten him thrown into jail for the time being. How would you feel if you were in such a situation? What scenery would clutter your mindscape? Would you be worried? Depressed? Bitter? Vindictive?

But he used this opportunity to write the most *joyful* of all his works. That's right: the most *joyful!* The person whose words we will study is Saul of Tarsus, otherwise known as Paul the apostle, and his words were written from a jail cell. Our primary source is found in the fourth chapter of Paul's letter to the Philippians. If there was anyone who knew the troubles of this life, it was Paul.

What are the prominent features of your mindscape right now? Would you characterize the vistas of your thought life as filled with peace and joy or with worry and fear? How are these thoughts impacting your life? Your health? Your relationships?

You might be thinking, *It's easy to say, "don't be anxious," but if I'm not supposed to have anxious, worried, or fearful thoughts, what am I going to think about?* Paul gives us a remarkable list of options. I'm sure this list is not exhaustive, but I'm also sure that these particular vistas are given to us by Paul, through the inspiration of the Holy Spirit, for a reason. Here they are:

> Whatever is true, whatever is noble, whatever
> is right, whatever is pure, whatever is lovely,
> whatever is admirable—if anything is excel-
> lent or praiseworthy—think about such things.
> (Philippians 4:8 NIV 1984)

These are the vistas we will be looking at together.
The expression "whatever" is often used as a throwaway
phrase of apathy or indecision. We say it when we really
don't know how to respond—and usually with more
than a hint of sarcasm! This usage of "whatever" has
been anointed as the most annoying expression in conversation for the past several years.[1] Paul, however, follows up his "whatevers" with content that can change
our mindscape and our lives. The words Paul uses
would have been familiar to his readers. They are the
vocabulary of the Greek philosophers and ethicists—
ethical standards to which his readers should aspire.

Some have suggested, because of its common
usage, Paul is merely encouraging his audience to at
least respect and live up to the pagan morality around
them. But this is not Paul's style at all. He has already
reminded the Philippians that their "citizenship is in
heaven, and from it we await a Savior, the Lord Jesus
Christ" (Philippians 3:20). In the words of Moises Silva,
"The idea that at this point in the letter Paul descends
from such heights and asks his brothers merely to act
like well-behaved citizens can hardly be taken seriously.
Given the context…we must understand Paul's list as
representing distinctively Christian virtues."[2]

The approach of this book will be to look at each of the vistas in the new mindscape one by one. As we proceed, there are a few principles you should keep in mind.

YOU CAN'T DO THIS YOURSELF

I suppose if you thought you could do this by yourself you wouldn't have picked up this book! But I want to emphasize up front that this is not a *self-help* book. Nor is this some new twist on Norman Vincent Peale's *Power of Positive Thinking* approach. Trying to deal with your worries by just thinking positive thoughts is about as helpful as one little boy's understanding of his father's attempt at encouragement. The little boy came home discouraged about math class. He said, "Dad, I think I'm going to fail my math quiz tomorrow." His dad said, "Son, you are a good student. You need to be more positive." The boy thought for a moment and said, "I'm *positive* that I'm going to fail my math quiz tomorrow!" Not very helpful.

On my way home from work the other day, traffic was backed up and I found myself behind a car covered with bumper stickers. Every cause imaginable was represented. But the bumper sticker that caught my attention had this quote from the late reggae singer Bob Marley, "Emancipate yourself from mental slavery. None but ourselves can free our minds." Sounds nice, doesn't it? But have you ever tried to free your own mind? Don't think about a pink elephant. The same thing happens so often when we try to break old thought patterns. We determine not to worry or to be jealous or angry or lustful … but there it is. How can we change? Where is our help? What is the key?

YOU NEED A NEW OPERATING SYSTEM

Computers are a great challenge for me. As long as they do what they're supposed to do I'm fine, but when something goes wrong I'm in big trouble. This is an even bigger problem when something happens with the operating system. Since the operating system runs all of the programs, when something happens to it the whole thing comes crashing down. "Virus" is used to refer to our physical health. But it seems that we hear about them just as frequently in reference to our computers. Computer viruses can be contracted through programs or even via email and can cause our operating systems to crash.

Think about the mind as your operating system. Our minds determine what we are going to say and what we are going to do. Our will to say or do is informed by our minds, and we engage the world on that basis. I've got some bad news for you: Our minds have a virus, and that virus is sin. This virus hasn't been "caught" from bad drinking water, another person's careless sneeze, or from an innocent-looking email, but is part of our being. After all, what do we mean when we say, "I'm only human," or "nobody's perfect?" We mean that imperfection and moral failure are characteristic of the human condition. How does this virus affect our minds? It starts with being determined to go our own way, not God's way. Since God made us and the whole universe, this really doesn't work out. But that doesn't stop us from trying. We are always wanting to be someone we aren't—God! We try to live like we are the center of the universe. The sad result of going our own way is that we are selfish, not selfless, toward other people. Sin has infected *everyone* including you, me, and everyone you know.

If you doubt that this virus is part of our operating system at birth, watch toddlers. Have you ever noticed that children's self-absorbed wills become obvious at a very early age? They say "no!" when told to do something and "mine!" when told to share. We often call this the "terrible twos." Why is this the case? I like to explain this time in life merely as the time that children's sinful natures learn to walk and talk. As we grow older we become more sophisticated about masking the "mines" and the "no's," but they're still there.

You might think that you sin only when you consciously do what you know is wrong (and of course that is sin!). But sin is more than an isolated incident in our lives. One of the Greek words translated "sin" is an archery term meaning, "to miss the mark." There are many ways that we miss God's mark, and we do so without even realizing it because every part of our world and ourselves is impacted by sin. Even our minds are impacted by sin. I promised that this was not going to be a theological tome, but you need to know one theological term before we go any further. Theologians refer to the *noetic* effect of sin. In other words, the impact of sin on the way we think. This word is a direct descendent of the word *nous,* the Greek term for "mind." Our sinful words and deeds have to come from somewhere. They come from the self-focused desires that fill our thoughts. They come from a sinful operating system. They come from self-involved, self-absorbed minds.

If you have any doubt about this, think about the Great Commandment given to us by Jesus, "You shall love the Lord your God with all your heart and with all your soul and *with all your mind*" (Matthew 22:37, emphasis added). Do you know anyone who loves the Lord with *all* his mind, *all* the time? I don't. This is why the Bible talks about the need for a transformed mind (Romans 12:1–2) and a renewed mind (Ephesians 4:34).

In reminding us about the Great Commandment, Jesus convicts us of the bad news of our great need. The good news is that he has done something that makes a new operating system possible. As the divine Son of God, he was the only person who *never* had a sinful thought. He lived in this world with all of the stress (and so much more) that we experience, but he never stopped trusting God. He never became paralyzed or self-absorbed. He was the only one who always loved the Lord with all his heart, soul, mind, and strength. But we must not make the mistake of thinking that the answer to our problem is to "be like Jesus"—because we can't. He was perfect. We are not. The reason Jesus came into the world was not merely to keep God's standards perfectly but to take the consequences for our sins. He did this through his death on the cross, where he not only paid the penalty for our sins, but broke the power of sin for all who will believe in him. The question we need to ask ourselves isn't "What would Jesus do?" but "What has Jesus done?"

Sin unaddressed is like a little dictator who insists on his own way. This dictator of our sinful nature is a slave-maker and, apart from the grace of God, we are stuck with the old mindscape with no hope of breaking free. Through faith Jesus forgives our sins and provides the power for a new way of thinking through the gift of his Spirit. As John Owen wrote many years ago, "There can be no greater evidence of a renewed heart and mind than a change in the habit and stream of our thoughts."[3]

Here is an important distinction to remember. While our forgiveness is instantaneous and complete when we believe, building a new mindscape is a *process* in which Jesus is at work in our lives over the long haul. When Paul speaks of our forgiveness, he uses "done-deal" language: "Therefore, since we have been justified by faith, we have peace with God through our Lord Jesus Christ" (Romans 5:1). The same idea is clearly seen in these words from John's first letter, "I am writing to you, little children, because your sins are forgiven for his name's sake" (1 John 2:12). All who believe in Jesus have the assurance that they are in right standing (justified) and have their sins forgiven. We are also assured that this establishes the beginning of something brand new in our experience. "Therefore, if anyone is in Christ, he is a new creation. The old has passed away; behold, the new has come" (2 Corinthians 5:17). The "new" also includes a new mindscape.

It is important to remember that the establishment of a new relationship with God through Jesus by faith is immediate, but the transformation of our lifestyle and way of thinking is not. We have been given a new operating system, but we are called upon to *use* it. Paul uses the analogy of changing our clothes to talk about the *process* of change that occurs in our lives, "in reference to your former manner of life, you lay aside the old self, which is being corrupted in accordance with the lusts of deceit, and that you be *renewed in the spirit of your mind*, and put on the new self, which in the likeness of God has been created in righteousness and holiness of the truth" (Ephesians 4:22–24 NASB, emphasis added). As you can see, this includes taking off the old way of thinking and putting on a new way of thinking. He puts it another way in the book of Romans. "Do not be conformed to this world, *but be transformed by the renewal of your mind*, that by testing you may discern what is the will of God, what is good and acceptable and perfect" (Romans 12:2, emphasis added). The word translated "transformed" is in the present tense. The transformation of your mindscape is an ongoing process. The word itself provides another picture for us. It is the word from which we get our word *metamorphosis*, which describes the process of the growth and development of an organism. When we hear this word, most of us think about the stages of the butterfly, from egg to caterpillar to pupa to adult. In every case the word *metamorphosis* is used to describe progress and growth.

This is what we should expect to experience in our new mindscape: a gradual progression and transformation in the way we think. The problem with the quick fixes of this self-help world is that they fail to address the most fundamental problem: our flawed operating system. I hope you can see that the answer to a transformed mindscape doesn't come from the outside in but through transformation from the inside out. This transformation occurs as we daily go to Jesus in faith and ask for his power to change, to listen, and to think differently. This leads us to another important principle.

A NEW MINDSCAPE LEADS
TO A NEW LIFESCAPE

As we look at each of the vistas of the new mindscape, we are going to see how important each one is to the way we live. The Lord's purpose is comprehensive and holistic with the goal of impacting not only the way that we think, but the way we live. The words of Paul immediately following the passage upon which we are focusing make this point. "What you have learned and received and heard and seen in me—*practice these things*, and the God of peace will be with you" (Philippians 4:9, emphasis added). When there is a change in the way we think, there will be a definite change in our words and actions as well. This will be one of the important bonus benefits of this study.

HOW WE WILL PROCEED

Are you ready to begin dismantling the old way of thinking? Are you tired of worrying about everything? Do you want to be finished with fear? Here's how we'll do it:

- First, we'll take a few moments to define each of the vistas in Philippians 4:8, by looking at the concept captured by the word Paul uses.

- Next, we'll look at the old mindscape and the troubles caused by the old way of thinking.
- Then, we'll take some time to observe and admire the new mindscape.
- Finally, we'll examine how this vista of the new mindscape impacts our new lifescape.

At the end of each chapter will also be a few questions (Food for Thought) to help you apply the principles discussed. There will also be suggested memory verses to help plant these principles in your minds.

2

What? Me Worry?

❧

"Worry is carrying a burden God never intended us to bear."

Author unknown

What's the biggest worry in your life right now? Are you worried about your financial circumstances; whether you will have enough to pay the mortgage, to retire, or just to buy the necessities of life? Perhaps you're worried about your children: their friends, their grades, their behavior, or their future? Health issues can also be very worrisome. Other stresses come from strained relationships with a family member, someone at work, or a friend.

Then there are just the hard circumstances of life. Sometimes bad things come out of nowhere, like a pink slip at work or when a car breaks down. At other times we can see difficulties coming and know that we will somehow have to get through them. When our son Nate was deployed to Iraq as a scout platoon commander at the height of the surge, we knew he was going to be in harm's way in a combat zone for fifteen months. Only those who have loved ones deployed can understand this particular burden.

We worry about little things. We worry about huge things. There are things we worry about for a few minutes and there are things that we worry about every day.

As we embark on developing a new mindscape, we must take a closer look at what to do *first* when the worries of life press in upon us. In order to do this we must step back and look at the verses that immediately precede Paul's description of a godly mindscape:

> Do not be anxious about anything, but in everything by prayer and supplication with thanksgiving let your requests be made known to God. And the peace of God, which surpasses all understanding, will guard your hearts and your minds in Christ Jesus. (Philippians 4:6–7)

I don't know about you, but whenever I hear absolute terms such as "always" or "never" it gives me pause. This is particularly true when someone complains about another person, saying that they "always" this or "never" that. When I hear these words in a counseling situation the speaker is usually (notice I didn't say always!) overstating the case.

In this passage, however, Paul uses absolute terminology. He writes that we should be anxious for *nothing.* In fact, in the Greek text the word translated "nothing" comes first for emphasis. To make his point even clearer, the word translated "be anxious" is in the imperative mood, giving "Be anxious for nothing" even more force! Paul is saying that we shouldn't worry about *anything . . . anything at all.* Was he some kind of Alfred E. Neuman ("What? Me Worry?"), or the precursor of Bobby McFerrin's "Don't Worry, Be Happy"? Was he advocating his contemporary stoics' acceptance of life's circumstances as fate?

All of us have worries and concerns. Let's call them "worry weeds" popping up in our mindscape. Paul says, "Be anxious for *nothing.* Don't worry about *anything.*" How is this possible?

Worry weeds are stubborn. If something isn't done they can overtake our whole mindscape and impact all that we do. Anyone who has driven in the southeastern United States has seen the kudzu plant. It was introduced to the United States in the late nineteenth century and has literally run wild. It covers more than seven million acres of the Southeast and can grow as fast as sixty feet per year. It all began innocently enough but by 1972 the USDA declared kudzu to be a weed!

Our worry weeds can begin to take over our minds the way kudzu is taking over parts of the United States. Worry can smother the joy right out of our lives as it shields us from the light of the truth of God's love for us. Today's anxiety immobilizes us as our thoughts get tangled in what might happen tomorrow. What can we do?

Lots of people suggest that to overcome worry we merely need to "believe in ourselves." Sounds noble but it just so happens that it is "me, myself, and I" who generates these worries and their very existence demonstrates my frailty and inability. To say that I should be able to handle it by myself when I am clearly *not* handling it by myself merely makes me worry that much more. Let's return now to what Paul says.

Paul follows his "be anxious for nothing" with an "everything." He writes, "but *in everything* by prayer and supplication with thanksgiving let your requests be made known to God." Paul isn't telling us to just "stop worrying." Instead, he is pointing us in a different direction. When we face circumstances that cause stress or anxiety—whatever they are—the first thing to do is to go to our heavenly Father and tell him about all of our troubles. Paul calls that "prayer." Prayer is the reset button we need to engage when things go wrong in life.

One day my television set just stopped working. I was frustrated because there was something I really wanted to watch. So I called my son-in-law, who is very savvy with technology. He said, "Just unplug it, wait a couple of minutes, and then plug it in again." I thought, "How could that be the answer?" Nonetheless, I took his advice and, *voila*, it worked! I have learned to try this with most gadgets and it works, more times than not. Of course our minds are not electronic gadgets that we can just unplug and reboot. So how does prayer work to "reset" our minds? "Everything" is an absolutely comprehensive term. We are to pray about *everything*—all of the worry weeds that spring up in our mindscape, everything on the short list we looked at above, and anything else that comes along. But how can prayer be such a powerful antidote to anxiety?

PRAYER PUTS THINGS
INTO PERSPECTIVE

On a recent trip Barb and I visited a beautiful property. One of the features on the grounds was a huge hedge maze consisting of lots of misleading turns and dead ends. It would really be easy to get lost in there. At the maze we visited, as at most similar mazes elsewhere, there was a tall platform overlooking the hedges. From this platform, an overseer could see the whereabouts of anyone in the maze. I'm sure it is there to give direction to someone who might panic as they are trying to find their way out.

Sometimes we too feel like we're in a maze and don't know which way to turn. We fear that if we take a wrong turn, it will lead to a dead end from which we might not be able to escape. When we're feeling lost and frustrated, the Lord knows our circumstances and is eager to direct us if we'll just ask him. Prayer puts us in touch with the One who sees the beginning from the end. The One who can give us his perspective on our worries and fears. The One who promises to never leave us or forsake us (Hebrews 13:5). The One on whom we can cast all of our cares because he cares for us (1 Peter 5:7).

Our verses from Philippians 4 also give us direction about the characteristics of prayer that smothers worry and how we can implement them:

Pray specifically. Paul uses different words for "prayer" in verse 6. The first is a general word for prayer, but the second word, "supplication," refers to an urgent *specific* plea. This is reinforced when he adds, "let your requests be made known to God." I've heard some folks say that when they pray they don't ask for anything for themselves. This might sound very selfless and holy, but it is wrong! The prayer Jesus taught his own disciples includes specific personal requests. It begins with praise to our Father in heaven and ends with his kingdom and power and glory; but in the middle supplications Jesus teaches us to ask God to meet our important personal needs. "Give us this day our daily bread, and forgive us our debts, as we also have forgiven our debtors. And lead us not into temptation, but deliver us from evil" (Matthew 6:11–13). Requests for daily provision, forgiveness, and protection are quite personal, and we are urged to bring them before the Lord regularly. This includes things we are prone to worry about. Do not be reluctant to cry out to the Lord about anything and everything.

Pray remembering God's goodness. You'll also notice that Paul tells us to pray "with thanksgiving." Praying with thanksgiving requires us to remember all of the good things the Lord has done for us and is doing for us now. After all, there are more things in your mind-scape than just worry weeds. Worries might be in the foreground at the moment, but there are many other things to which you should draw your attention and for which you should be thankful. This isn't easy because our natural tendency is to focus on our worries rather than to give thanks. When you are worried, bring your cares to the Lord, but also remember his kindness and goodness to you right now and in the past.

Pray expecting an answer. Another reason we can pray with thanksgiving is that we can expect an answer. Sometimes the answer might not be what we expect, but the Lord has promised to answer. As many have observed, the answers the Lord gives can be "yes," "no," or "not yet." We might always like a "yes" but the Lord our heavenly Father knows what is best and he will not give us something that isn't good for us. When I was in college I thought the Lord's plan for me was to become a famous tuba performer. Yes, that's right—I said, a tuba performer! He had given me lots of success up to that point and I was a performance major in my college. I decided that I would audition for the United States Marine Band (The President's Own) in Washington, DC, and the Curtis Institute in Philadelphia. I didn't make either one. It was "no" and "no" from the Lord. I was disappointed, but in closing those two doors the Lord was directing me elsewhere—toward the ministry.

Pray expecting that God will want your response, too. As we pray, the Lord might make it clear that there is something that we need to *do*. For example, if you're worried about a relationship, God might lead you to have a conversation with the individual with whom you've had difficulties. He will certainly impress upon you the need to look for and apply for jobs if you have lost your job. New health challenges will require a change in diet, exercise, and lifestyle. Be ready to be directed toward things you might need to *do* regarding your situation. This leading will always be according to and consistent with his Word. If you feel that God is calling you to do something that is beyond you—pray about that as well. If he is calling you to do something, he will also give you his Spirit to do it. Pray for the Spirit to help you and direct you so that you can follow Jesus wherever he calls you to go. Fundamentally, Paul reminds us that the Lord will answer, and that we should be prepared for where that answer may lead or what that answer may call us to do.

PRAYER LEADS TO PEACE

Paul tells us that the result of our prayer is that "the peace of God, which surpasses all understanding, will guard your hearts and your minds in Christ Jesus." Notice that this doesn't promise that the problems will go away, but that even in the midst of our problems, anxiety can be replaced by peace.

There are a couple of very interesting characteristics of this peace. It is *incomprehensible*. Paul writes that "it surpasses all understanding." This means it can't be explained from a merely human perspective. The presence of peace in the midst of adversity is a gift from God and is difficult to explain. John MacArthur describes it this way:

> True spiritual peace is completely different from the superficial, ephemeral, fragile human peace. It is the deep, settled confidence that all is well between the soul and God because of His loving, sovereign control of one's life both in time and eternity. That calm assurance is based on the knowledge that sins are forgiven, blessing is present, good is abundant even in trouble, and heaven is ahead. The peace that God gives His beloved children as their possession and privilege has nothing to do with the circumstances of life.[1]

Some years ago a dear family in our congregation lost their precious fourteen-year-old daughter to a previously undetected heart disorder known as long QT syndrome. Lacey's death was completely unexpected, as she collapsed while running with some friends just two days before Christmas. Everyone was stunned and concerned about how her mother and dad would respond. As followers of Christ, even in the midst of this tragedy, they had peace. It was a calmness and tranquility of spirit that perplexed many. Certainly their hearts were broken and they grieved deeply, but they had a peace that was truly beyond ability to explain in any other way than that it was from the Lord.

Our friends were somewhat of an oddity to those who did not know the Lord; the peace the Lord provided surpassed the understanding of many observers. Those of us who believed understood how the Lord was providing for them. They have continued to trust him with their ongoing grief through the years. The Lord is the Good Shepherd who walks with his sheep through the valley of the shadow of death. Lacey's mother once told me that the valleys of grief continue to come, but they are less frequent and not as deep. Grief is a long dark valley and while the tears still come, the promise is that one day "He will wipe away every tear from their eyes, and death shall be no more, neither shall there be mourning, nor crying, nor pain anymore, for the former things have passed away" (Revelation 21:4).

The peace that the Lord gives provides *protection*. Paul writes in Philippians 4:7 that the Lord's peace "will guard your hearts and minds." As he wrote these words, Paul was in a Roman prison and could look right at the soldier charged to keep him safely in protective custody. As Martyn Lloyd-Jones wrote:

> It conjures up a picture. What will happen is that this peace of God will walk round the ramparts and towers of our life. We are inside, and the activities of the heart and mind are producing those stresses and anxieties and strains from the outside. But the peace of God will keep them all out and we ourselves inside will be at perfect peace.[2]

It is in times of difficulty that we need his protection over our hearts and minds. The enemy of our souls is all too eager to whisper into our ears that "the Lord can't love you if he allowed this to happen to you" and other such lies. The Lord's peace guards us against the bitterness and cynicism that can blow us off course if we are not anchored in his loving promise of peace.

Finally, please note that Paul writes that all of this is "in Christ Jesus," who is the Prince of Peace and the one in whom all of the promises of God are "yes and amen" (2 Corinthians 1:20). He came to sympathize with our weaknesses. In fact, he was one who "in every respect has been tempted as we are, yet without sin" (Hebrews 4:15). His death on the cross for our sins and resurrection from the dead paved the way so that all who believe in him can "with confidence draw near to the throne of grace, that we may receive mercy and find grace to help in time of need" (Hebrews 4:16). Times of trial are times of need. Things to worry about are things we should pray about.

I recall as a little boy walking up the street to visit my godly Grandma Witmer. She was a faithful follower of the Lord. She never owned a television set but her radio was usually tuned into the local Christian radio station. I will never forget the catchy theme song of one of her favorite programs. I don't remember the name of the program but the theme song began with the lyrics "Why worry when you can pray? Trust Jesus, he'll lead the way. Don't be a doubting Thomas; trust fully in his promise. Why worry, worry, worry, worry, when you can pray?"

I wasn't a follower of Jesus at the time, so the song seemed very corny though it was catchy. Now I have come to see the great wisdom in its words. This is exactly what Paul teaches us to do. What is the first thing we need to do when troubles strike? Be anxious for nothing. Start to pray. Prayer is a weed killer of the greatest strength and can fight off the worry weeds before they overrun your mindscape. Don't be surprised if you sense a peace that might not "make sense," given the circumstances in which you find yourself. This is a gift from the Lord grounded in his grace in Christ Jesus. As John Owen wrote in his work, *Spiritual Mindedness*, "Prayer stirs up the inward spiritual springs of which flow faith and love. Prayer arouses holy thoughts of God and of spiritual things."

As we move on to the next chapter, we will face the very practical point that when you have challenges and problems in your life you can't pray *all the time*. Thus, we will next consider what we're supposed to think about when we're not worrying or praying. These principles will help transform your mindscape.

FOOD FOR THOUGHT

1. What things do you worry about most on a regular basis? What are you worrying about today?

2. Has worrying helped the situation? Why or why not? How have your worries impacted you?

3. How motivated or reluctant are you to pray about the situations you face? In either case, why?

4. Can you think of a time when you experienced "peace beyond comprehension?" If so, describe it now. If not, what's a situation in which you'd *like* to experience God's peace?

5. When you pray, how willing are you to accept a "no" or "not yet" from the Lord? Explain your answer.

6. Make a list of the worry weeds in your mindscape right now. Then, pray specifically for the Lord's help. Don't forget to listen for some things that you might need to *do*.

MEMORY VERSES

Philippians 4:6-8: "Do not be anxious about anything, but in everything, by prayer and petition, with thanksgiving, present your requests to God. And the peace of God, which transcends all understanding, will guard your hearts and your minds in Christ Jesus. Finally, brothers, whatever is true, whatever is noble, whatever is right, whatever is pure, whatever is lovely, whatever is admirable—if anything is excellent or praiseworthy—think about such things" (NIV 1984).

3

Whatever Is True

⤜

"Truth renews the mind. Indeed, the truth which would affect the heart, which moves the heart, which changes the heart, must first enter through the vestibule of the mind if it would enter the sanctuary of the heart."

John Armstrong[1]

There's nothing like a good courtroom scene. One of the most dramatic in all of cinema was in the film *A Few Good Men*. Jack Nicholson played the tough Colonel Nathan Jessup who has been accused of ordering a "code red" that led to the death of one of his Marines. Tom Cruise played the smart-alecky young naval lawyer Daniel Kaffee who was charged with the defense of the young Marines who were accused of perpetrating the crime. The climax of the film depicted

Cruise's final cross-examination. He gets right into Jessup's face demanding the truth, to which the witness explodes, "You can't handle the truth!"

Can *you* handle the truth? What place should truth have in your mindscape?

We have seen that the first thing we need to do when faced with the challenges of life is to press the reset button and pray. Looking to the Lord gives us peace in the midst of the storms of life. Did you ever notice how your mind gets fixated on your worries? And you just keep going over and over the same terrain? Bringing those worries to your heavenly Father will begin to release you from being stuck in the same old way of thinking. But what do we replace our worried thoughts with? Paul begins his list of the vistas of a new mindscape with this: "whatever is true."

Truth is the most important vista in our new way of thinking, because everything else flows from it. To use another analogy, truth is the cornerstone to which every other stone must be oriented in order for the building to rise with integrity. Get this one wrong and there will be nothing but trouble the rest of the way. A great challenge that we face is identifying *what is true*. According to a dictionary definition, that which is true is "in accordance with the actual state or conditions; conforming to reality or fact."[2] But there seems to be disagreement these days over where to find what conforms to actual reality or fact.

In two national surveys conducted by Barna Research—one among adults and one among teenagers—people were asked if they believe that there are moral absolutes that are unchanging or whether moral truth is relative to the circumstances. By a nearly three-to-one margin (sixty-four percent versus twenty-two percent), adults said truth is always relative to the person and their situation. The perspective was even more lopsided among teenagers, eighty-three percent said moral truth depends on the circumstances, and only six percent said moral truth is absolute.[3]

This is the foundation of the "it might be true for you but it's not true for me" mentality. The bottom line is that something is either true or it is not true. Otherwise, people just make things up as they go along. This is what we call "relativism." As David Wells has written:

> Truth is now simply a matter of etiquette: it has no authority, no sense of rightness, because it is no longer anchored in anything absolute. If it persuades, it does so only because our experience has given it its persuasive power, but tomorrow our experience might be different.[4]

Let's face it: People come up with their ideas of what is true from many different sources. Certainly our parents, our friends, and the broader culture around us have influenced us. But these are not always reliable sources of what is true. For example, some ideas and practices that cultures literally outlawed in the past are now embraced and celebrated.

But is truth really determined by popular consensus? I think we can agree that something cannot be true and not true at the same time. Philosophers call this the law of noncontradiction. Take a moment to consider the *source* of what you think about life. Why do you think what you think? Why do you believe what you believe? Are you confident that you can trust your sources? Perhaps one of the reasons your mindscape is in turmoil is that you are not certain about what is true or where it can be found.

Paul had no doubt whatsoever about the source of truth. When he refers to what is true, he is referring to that which has been revealed by the living God who is the God of truth. "For Paul the truth is narrowly circumscribed, finding its measure in God (Rom. 1:18, 25) and the Gospel (Gal. 2:5; 5:7)."[5] God is the *source* of truth. "This God—his way is perfect; the word of the LORD proves true; he is a shield for all those who take refuge in him" (Psalm 18:30). It is the revelation of his Word that serves us as the *standard* for what is true. "The sum of your word is truth, and every one of your righteous rules endures forever" (Psalm 119:160).

As John Armstrong has written, "Truth is an inevitable expression of our concern with God—God who is the measure of all things, who reveals to us His mind. He reveals His mind to us in the words of sacred Scripture so that we might hear and understand the mind of God."[6] This is the claim of the Scriptures from cover to cover. His Word certainly meets the definition of truth as "conformity to reality or fact." In the Scriptures we meet the one who is truth incarnate, truth in the flesh. He is the one described by John as "full of grace and truth" (John 1:14). He described himself as "the way, and the truth, and the life" (John 14:6). Do you want to see what truth looks like in person? Study the life and words of Jesus. When Jesus stood trial Pilate proposed the question, "What is truth?" Little did the Roman governor know that the very incarnation of truth was standing right before his very eyes. Let's take a few moments and consider some realities revealed in the Scriptures.

THE TRUTH ABOUT GOD

If your view of God is derived from popular culture, you might think that the divine being is merely an impersonal force along the lines of *Star Wars*; or George Burns playing God with a stinking stogie stuck in his mouth in *Oh, God*; or Morgan Freeman in both *Bruce Almighty* and *Evan Almighty*. But when you look to the source of truth in Scripture, you see an awesome picture of one God in three persons (Father, Son, and Holy Spirit) who in his omnipotence created the universe merely by commanding it into being with his Word (Genesis 1:1).

As our creator, he is the One to whom "each of us will give an account of himself" (Romans 14:12). That wouldn't be so bad except for the fact that God is perfectly holy and righteous and cannot endure the presence of sin. Had he not reached out to help us in our great need, that would really be something to worry about! God's response to our need shows his attributes of love and grace as he "so loved the world, that he gave his only Son, that whoever believes in him should not perish but have eternal life" (John 3:16). All who have faith in the Son have a foundation upon which to live life now, and the promise of eternal life forever. This is true and something to think about when life gets tough. How does knowing this truth about God change the way you are thinking about your life right now? Will he who created you, who counts the hairs of your head, who cares for you as a Father cares for his children, also not be with you in the midst of all of your difficulties?

Let's think about how meditating on some of the characteristics of God helps us with the worry weeds in our mindscape. Theologians call these God's "attributes." These are the sturdy truths that, as we remind ourselves of them, will transform our worried thoughts into confidence that our heavenly Father has not forgotten us and will never leave us or forsake us.

When you are weak and insecure, think about the truth that *God is all powerful (omnipotent).* "Be exalted, O Lord, in your strength! We will sing and praise your power" (Psalm 21:13). Remember he created the universe merely by calling it into being with his word. He provides strength to those who trust in him.

I can't begin to tell you how many times I have stood beside individuals afflicted with an illness that would eventually take their lives, who nonetheless found their strength in the Lord. As Paul wrote elsewhere, "Though our outer self is wasting away, our inner self is being renewed day by day" (2 Corinthians 4:16).

Just a few verses after describing the vistas of the new mindscape Paul writes, "I can do all things through him who strengthens me" (Philippians 4:13). On another occasion Paul was struck with a physical affliction and prayed that the Lord would remove it. What was the Lord's answer?

> But he said to me, "My grace is sufficient for you, for my power is made perfect in weakness." Therefore I will boast all the more gladly of my weaknesses, so that the power of Christ

> may rest upon me. For the sake of Christ, then, I am content with weaknesses, insults, hardships, persecutions, and calamities. For when I am weak, then I am strong. (2 Corinthians 12:9–10)

There is no need to worry when you are weak because this is when the Lord's strength will shine through! Paul was used by the Lord to heal many others, but in this case he had the opportunity to experience the Lord's power when he felt powerless. In your weakness there is another reason to rest in the Lord. The truth is that as one of Christ's sheep you are completely and eternally secure.

> My sheep hear my voice, and I know them, and they follow me. I give them eternal life, and they will never perish, and no one will snatch them out of my hand. My Father, who has given them to me, is greater than all, and no one is able to snatch them out of the Father's hand. (John 10:27–29)

When things are changing and in turmoil all around you, what a comfort it is to know your relationship with him is unshakeable as you are completely secure in his strong hand.

When you are confused, remember that *the Lord knows everything (omniscient).* Have you ever come to an intersection and not known which way to turn? The problem is that there are cars behind you eager for you to make up your mind—you *have* to decide. Perhaps you have come to a crossroads in your life and it's not clear which job to take or which direction to go in a relationship. The people around you are confident in what you should do, but you aren't. Or perhaps you've made a painstaking decision but now doubt yourself. These are the types of situations that can lead to lots of worry. But what do you do? Trust in your all-wise God. "The LORD by wisdom founded the earth; by understanding he established the heavens" (Proverbs 3:19). He created everything and knows everything! He knows everything about your situation, too, and has promised to give you direction and wisdom if you will ask. "If any of you lacks wisdom, let him ask God, who gives generously to all without reproach, and it will be given him" (James 1:5). Making this truth part of your mindscape will remind you to ask him for guidance when you need it. The truth is that he will show you the way.

When you are lonely, the truth is that *God is everywhere (omnipresent)*. Perhaps you've lost your spouse of many years and suddenly find yourself alone. Maybe you're a single parent who, after your children are asleep, feel isolated and on your own. Remember, wherever you are, he is with you. "Where shall I go from your Spirit? Or where shall I flee from your presence? If I ascend to heaven, you are there! If I make my bed in Sheol [the realm of the dead], you are there! If I take the wings of the morning and dwell in the uttermost parts of the sea, even there your hand shall lead me, and your right hand shall hold me" (Psalm 139:7–10). This is really bad news for those who are pretending that God doesn't exist, because there is no escaping his presence. But if you trust in him the good news is that he is *always* with you. You are *never* alone. "So do not fear, for I am with you; do not be dismayed, for I am your God. I will strengthen you and help you; I will uphold you with my righteous right hand" (Isaiah 41:10 NIV). Though people abandon you, the truth is that he is with you.

When resources are running low, the truth is that the Lord created everything and that *everything belongs to him.* He has also promised to provide for your needs. Every one of God's sheep can exclaim with confidence "The LORD is my shepherd; I shall not want" (Psalm 23:1 KJV).

A few verses after Paul's description of the new mindscape he reminds his readers, "my God will meet all your needs according to his glorious riches in Christ Jesus" (Philippians 4:19 NIV). What a great promise. Notice that Paul hasn't promised that God will provide everything that you *want* but everything that you *need.* Jesus also addressed this worry weed in the Sermon on the Mount:

> Therefore I tell you, do not be anxious about your life, what you will eat or what you will drink, nor about your body, what you will put on. Is not life more than food, and the body more than clothing? Look at the birds of the air: they neither sow nor reap nor gather into barns, and yet your heavenly Father feeds them. Are you not of more value than they? And which of you by being anxious can add a single hour to his span of life? And why are you anxious about clothing? Consider the lilies of the field, how they grow: they neither toil nor spin, yet I

tell you, even Solomon in all his glory was not arrayed like one of these. But if God so clothes the grass of the field, which today is alive and tomorrow is thrown into the oven, will he not much more clothe you, O you of little faith? Therefore do not be anxious, saying, 'What shall we eat?' or 'What shall we drink?' or 'What shall we wear?' For the Gentiles seek after all these things, and your heavenly Father knows that you need them all. But seek first the kingdom of God and his righteousness, and all these things will be added to you. (Matthew 6:25–33)

There are a couple of realities from these verses to consider. First, you are loved by the Lord and he will take care of you. Second, it is important to keep your priorities in order to be assured of this promise. "Seek first the kingdom of God and his righteousness, and all these things will be added to you." Keeping the Lord and his ways in first place in your life is essential to living in the assurance that he will provide for you. If you find yourself drifting from that truth, if you find yourself seeking everything *except* the kingdom of God, turn to Jesus and ask for forgiveness and help. He wants to work in you the very things that he commands you to do. The truth is that he loves you and provides for you—not only in times of pressing need but all the time.

When you are doubtful, remember that *the Lord is good*. A mealtime prayer that many remember begins "God is great. *God is good.*" Sometimes when things go wrong, terribly wrong, you might question whether

God is really a good God. You might even be thinking that somehow he might be out to "get you." The truth is that God is good.

David wrote Psalm 34 when he was in a heap of trouble. In spite of his mistakes and sins, the Lord delivered him, and in response David wrote, "Oh, taste and see that *the LORD is good*! Blessed is the man who takes refuge in him!" (Psalm 34:8, emphasis added). Jesus is the Good Shepherd. This means that his interest is for the good and well-being of his sheep. Do not allow the troubles you experience make you question the goodness of God.

I would encourage you to search the Bible and learn more about God. The Bible is his authorized autobiography! As you fill your mind with the truth of God, you will notice that your worries and anxieties no longer have a stranglehold on your life. Yes, life remains hard, but the certain truth of God's presence, his love, and his help begins to fill your mind with hope even in the midst of trouble and sorrow.[7]

THE TRUTH ABOUT YOU

The Scriptures also reveal the truth about you. First of all, you are not just a hunk of living matter but you are made in the image of God (Genesis 1:26–27). You are a rational being because he is a rational being. You are a spiritual being because God is spirit. Your soul is eternal because you are made in his image.

However, though you are created in his image, he is still the Creator and you are a creature. Don't make the mistake that Morgan Freeman made when interviewed about roles he has played, including God. Take a look at this (emphasis added below):

> **Interviewer:** Do you think there is a God?
> **Morgan Freeman:** Do I think there's a God? Um (pause) yeah.
> **Interviewer:** You paused.
> **Morgan Freeman:** I paused because I am God.

He was asked to clarify by the dumbfounded interviewer:

> **Interviewer:** Because every man is created in God's image.
> **Morgan Freeman:** Yes or God's created in my image.[8]

As much as I respect Mr. Freeman's acting skills, his words reveal a distorted mindscape that many people share, that they are somehow not only lord of their own lives, but also lords of reality in general. The problem with this way of thinking is that it isn't grounded in reality. Neither Morgan Freeman, you, nor I are God. We didn't create ourselves, choose the day of our birth, nor will we choose the day of our death. Deep inside we know we aren't God. Pretending we are fuels our anxiety and fears as we try to do the impossible—control those things that cannot be controlled by anyone but the Creator of the world.

Second, we are made in the image of God but that image has been blurred by sin. Compared to God's righteous standard of perfection we have all fallen short. We can still function but things aren't quite as they should be.

There is a cabin in the woods that our family has traveled to every summer of our lives (beginning with my parents in 1946). It is quite a rustic place that is easily more than one hundred years old. Most everything in the cabin "works" but it's not quite "right." For example, it has running water, but you can't drink it. It has an indoor bathroom in the basement, but there is no hot water. If you want to bathe, you heat water on the stove because there is no shower. There is a refrigerator, but it freezes items if placed too far back on the shelves. The owners bought a used microwave a few years ago, but the display doesn't work. There is a well, but the pump sometimes malfunctions and has to be reset.

This reminds me of our natural human condition. Everything "works" but it's not quite right. This is the impact of sin on our lives. As we saw earlier to say, "I'm only human" is not a statement of glorious autonomy but rather a universally accepted expression of human frailty and inability. This is a very important reality to embrace because it leads to an appropriate humility before the Lord and other people. You are not always right. You are not perfect. It's not always someone else's fault. When we are honest with ourselves, we struggle with guilt and the fear and worry that are attached to the things we know we should not have done and the things we should have done that we failed to do. Guilt becomes another way for worry to fill our minds.

The good news is that the Lord himself in the gift of his Son, the Lord Jesus Christ, has addressed our frail sinful condition. It is through him that the worry weed of guilt has been addressed.

"As far as the east is from the west, so far does he remove our transgressions from us" (Psalm 103:12). How far is the east from the west? They never meet, and that is the point! In speaking of the new covenant that is ours through Jesus, the Lord promised through Jeremiah the prophet: "I will forgive their iniquity, and I will remember their sin no more" (Jeremiah 31:34). Your mindscape should include a sober understanding of your own human mortality, frailty, and inability— but also what the Lord has done, and is doing, for you.

Finally, you did not come into this world through a random series of events; your existence was planned by the Lord. There is a purpose for your life. "'For I know the plans I have for you,' declares the LORD, 'plans to prosper you and not to harm you, plans to give you hope and a future'" (Jeremiah 29:11 NIV). Ultimately, your purpose is to bring glory to him.

ENEMIES OF TRUTH

There are certain adversaries of truth that can creep into your mindscape of which you must be aware. They will counter the impact of truth in your life. Let's take a look at just a couple of them:

Falsehood. Earlier we looked at the definition of "true." There was something I left out. Here is the complete definition with the previous omission included and italicized: "being in accordance with the actual state or conditions; conforming to reality or fact; *not false.*"[9] To assert that there is truth assumes the existence of that which is false. Falsehood fails to conform to reality or fact.

Falsehood began back in the garden when the serpent contradicted God's truth. He began by creating doubt in Eve's mind: "Did God actually say, 'You shall not eat of any tree in the garden'?" (Genesis 3:1). Eve asserted that God told them that they would die if they ate from the tree that was in the midst of the garden. This opened the door for Satan's direct contradiction of God's Word. "You will not surely die" (Genesis 3:4), he assured them. This was the very first misrepresentation of truth, the very first lie. The results were devastating, as spiritual death came upon not only the first couple but upon the whole human race. This is the reason that Jesus refers to Satan as the "father of lies" (John 8:44). The denial of truth is now a regular way of life among humans.

In an article entitled "Why We Lie," the *Wall Street Journal* didn't even need to bother to convince its readers that people are dishonest. "What we have found, in a nutshell: Everybody has the capacity to be dishonest, and almost everybody cheats—just by a little…. Except for a few outliers at the top and bottom, the behavior of almost everyone is driven by two opposing motivations. On the one hand, we want to benefit from cheating and get as much money and glory as possible; on the other hand, we want to view ourselves as honest, honorable people. Sadly, it is this kind of small-scale mass cheating, not the high-profile cases, that is most corrosive to society."[10]

How can you tell the difference between truth and falsehood? The best thing you can do is immerse yourself in the truth of God's Word so that falsehood will be more easily detected. The old story about agents who seek to stop counterfeiters applies here. What do you think federal agents study most to stop counterfeiters; real currency or counterfeit currency? They study *genuine* currency so they will be able to spot a fake easily in contrast to what they know about the real thing.

The Secret Service gives the following advice to US citizens that they can help in catching counterfeiters: "You can help guard against the threat from counterfeiters *by becoming more familiar with United States currency.* Look at the money you receive. *Compare a suspect note with a genuine note* of the same denomination and series, paying attention to the quality of printing and paper characteristics. Look for differences, not similarities" (emphasis added).[11] The best way to guard against falsehood is to become very familiar with the truth. There are lots of things that might seem right or correct, but they aren't right at all.

A few years ago, the American Dialect Society chose the word "truthiness" for its word of the year. What in the world is "truthiness?" "Truthiness refers to the quality of preferring concepts or facts one wishes to be true, rather than concepts or facts known to be true."[12] It might be comforting in the short term to embrace a foggy view of things, but it is always best to ally oneself with reality. Do all that you can to rid your mindscape of falsehood and truthiness (which is really falsehood in disguise). This leads to another enemy of truth.

Denial. Denial is the attempt to cover up and ignore the truth. This is how our problems began back in the garden, when the first couple clearly denied what their

Creator said about the consequences of eating the fruit of the tree of the knowledge of good and evil. In the book of Romans, Paul describes denial as a fundamental characteristic of those without faith: they "suppress the truth in unrighteousness" (Romans 1:18 NASB). If truth is always a reflection of reality, living in denial means failing to face up to the truth about something, whatever it might be.

Why do we sometimes live in denial? Because sometimes, the truth hurts. But living through the "hurt" that the truth inflicts begins the path to healing and wholeness.

Some years ago I was diagnosed with a mitral valve prolapse, a leaky valve. I was told it was a common problem and I shouldn't worry about it unless I became symptomatic. Sometime later I began experiencing symptoms, including shortness of breath and difficulty breathing when I would lie down at night. In fact, as the symptoms got worse I had to sleep in my recliner because I couldn't breathe lying down. I slept there for weeks. I went from doctor to doctor and even to the emergency room, where I received several diagnoses. It was a virus. It was pneumonia. None of these reflected the reality of the situation. To be honest with you, I was happy they weren't suggesting it was anything serious. But deep inside, I knew it *was* serious, because the symptoms were getting worse every day. Without the proper diagnosis (the truth!), I would not get the proper treatment.

Finally, I went to a new cardiologist who prescribed the appropriate test, which identified that my mitral valve had blown wide open. He described my heart as about as effective as a heater trying to heat a house with all the windows wide open. The diagnosis came on a Friday morning, and first thing next Monday morning, I had open-heart surgery. It was only after I had gotten the proper diagnosis that I could receive the proper treatment. Though I was told I needed immediate surgery, I was relieved because someone had finally gotten to the truth of the matter.

One of our church members, John, recently came up to me and said, "I'll never forget the first question I asked you when I came to Crossroads Church." I was embarrassed because I had forgotten, so I asked, "What was it?" He said, "I asked you 'Can God change a drunk?'" Of course my answer was, "Yes, through the power of the gospel." This was the beginning of a much longer conversation that has lasted several years. When John came to us, he was homeless and dependent on alcohol. Through the power of the gospel his life has changed. He has a wife and a home and ushers at the 8:30 service! The key was that he stopped deceiving himself and faced the reality that he was "a drunk"—a drunk who needed to be changed.[13]

Denial is an unwillingness to see the reality of the situation. Are there areas of your life in which you're denying the truth? Are you denying that you're addicted to a substance or to material that's destroying you? Are you in denial that *you* are the problem in your relationship with your spouse, your children, or your parents? Are you denying that you are crossing dangerous boundaries in your thoughts and in your behavior? Are you willing to continue enduring and perpetuating the pain, instead of admitting the truth? Admission of the truth is the beginning of the path to healing. It might be a long path to wholeness but at least you will be headed in the right direction.

FROM MINDSCAPE TO LIFESCAPE

Think about the difference that a mindscape filled with truth will make in your life! In the Scriptures, as we saw earlier, the Lord is the God of truth, and Jesus is described as full of grace and truth. His people are called to be people of truth. In our relationships, truth is the foundation of trust.

A good way to tell if you're a person of truth is to ask yourself if those closest to you at home and at work *trust* you. Does your spouse trust you? If not, ask yourself how you might have shaded the truth in your words or actions. Do your children trust you? If not, ask yourself if you've broken any promises to them. Why should they believe you now if you haven't followed through in the past? If they don't trust you, then there is a problem with truth in your lifescape. Are you known as a trustworthy employee where you work? If you are, it is because you're a person of truth whose life and performance on the job can be trusted.

Now, would you allow the light into your mindscape to consider this question: Might some of the worries that you have right now be the result of the damage of a breach of trust in your relationships with your spouse, with a child, with a parent, with a friend, or with your boss? If you're not truthful with others, you will not be trusted, and truth is the foundation of a genuine relationship. One of the most important things you can do is to go to that person and humbly (*and truthfully*) admit your departure from truth in word or deed. Ask forgiveness and commit to be truthful in the future, with this confession as a down payment. You should have realistic expectations going into the conversation, understanding that trust takes time to rebuild, one conversation and one interaction at a time. But it is worth being known as a person of truth!

Paul mentions, "whatever is true" first because everything else depends on your understanding of truth. As a mason orients every other stone to the cornerstone, so your understanding of truth will guide everything that follows in your mindscape.

Knowing and believing the truth about God and about you is foundational to fighting worry and anxiety.

FOOD FOR THOUGHT

1. In your own words, why is truth foundational to your mindscape? And how foundational is it in your life right now? Explain your answer.

2. Take time to think about the influences that exist in your life. What are the sources of your convictions about the truth? How reliable are they?

3. What areas of your life, if any, do you have in which you're living in denial? Be honest! (Maybe you should ask your spouse or a trusted friend to help you with this one.)

4. How does meditating on "whatever is true" help relieve the worries in your mindscape? When have you experienced this truth?

5. Which truth about God helps you the most with the particular worry weed you're struggling with right now? Why?

6. Can you honestly say that your family trusts you? Your boss? Your friends? If you even hesitate for a moment, take some time to think about what compromises of truth may have impacted that trust and how you can address it—now.

MEMORY VERSE

Psalm 25:5: "Lead me in your truth and teach me, for you are the God of my salvation; for you I wait all the day long."

4

Whatever Is Noble

"Oh, how great peace and quietness would he possess, who did cut off all vain anxiety… and place all his hope in God."

Thomas à Kempis[1]

As we continue our walk through a new mindscape that helps us counter our worries and anxieties, we move from "whatever is *true*" to "whatever is *noble*." The word that Paul uses (*semna*) is a little difficult to get a handle on. It is a word that was common in the Greek literature of his day but not used very often in the New Testament. One writer said, "It has such a richness about it that it is impossible to equate it with any one English word."[2] As one translation source noted:

It is difficult to find a good word for the adjective rendered "noble". This fact is reflected in the diverse translations: honest, honorable, worthy, deserving respect." Another possibility is "dignified," since this adjective is often used in that sense. Can be expressed in a phrase such as "that which causes people to look up" or "that which causes people's eyes to admire."[3]

Rienecker and Rogers, in their *Linguistic Key to the Greek New Testament*, add that "it implies that which is majestic and awe-inspiring."[4] This idea coincides with how it was often used in the literature of the day. It was often used to describe gods and deities who were "lofty and lifted up." This includes the concept of a majestic reign. As we seek to fill the vista of "whatever is noble" in our mindscape we need to ask ourselves, "What fills the bill of that which is 'lofty and lifted up' and 'that which causes people to look up' and the idea of 'majestic reign?'"

What causes you to look up? Usually we look up at something bigger than we are: the mountains, the ocean, a sky filled with stars. Why do we enjoy looking up? For many people, including me, there come a calmness and peace when we realize not only that God is bigger than everything that he made but that he is also bigger than all our problems, worries, and fears. We've already seen how studying the truth about God can help counter certain worry weeds in our mindscape. Now we're going to focus more specifically on looking up at God, who is exalted and reigns over everything, everywhere, all the time.

Another way to express this is to say that God is "sovereign." To be sovereign is to exercise "supreme rank, power, or authority."[5] Of course, there are earthly sovereigns—kings, queens, presidents and prime ministers—but their reign cannot compare with the reign of the Lord. This is beautifully expressed in these words of David, "Yours is the kingdom, O LORD, and you are exalted as head above all. Both riches and honor come from you, and you rule over all. In your hand are power and might, and in your hand it is to make great and to give strength to all" (1 Chronicles 29:11–12). Let's take a look at what God's sovereign reign means to you and how that meaning can transform your mindscape.

HE REIGNS EVERYWHERE

The Lord reigns *everywhere*—not only on this planet, but also over the entire universe! "Let the heavens be glad, and let the earth rejoice, and let them say among the nations, 'The LORD reigns!'" (1 Chronicles 16:31). There is no place over which God does not reign. "The LORD has established his throne in heaven, and his kingdom rules over all" (Psalm 103:19).

This means that God's right of rule extends over your life, your home, and your workplace. There is no place where you or a loved one can be out of his view or away from his care. This is of particular comfort when you are prone to worry about a loved one who may be absent from you. I mentioned earlier that our son Nate was deployed in Iraq as part of Operation Iraqi Freedom.

Many times we had no idea where he was located as he was out on various missions. As you might imagine, this led to quite a few anxious moments. I recall sitting in our living room during those days. Sometimes when I would hear a car door close outside, I would pray that the next thing I heard would not be the doorbell rung by uniformed visitors. As we would walk through our day, we would wonder where Nate was or what he might be doing. When he was out on missions, we would not hear from him for weeks at a time. On one occasion, the phone rang and we were surprised to hear Nate's voice. He was hunkered down at a combat outpost but was able to call us on a satellite phone. It was the middle of the night there. We were comforted to hear his voice until we heard helicopters in the background—followed by Nate saying, "Got to run!"

I cannot begin to tell you what a comfort it was during those fourteen months to know that the Lord was there in the combat zone, watching over Nate. If you happen to visit me in my seminary office, you will see one-half of a one-hundred-dollar bill set in plexiglass on my desk. It has caught the attention of many visitors. Shortly before Nate left for Iraq I took out a hundred-dollar bill and tore it in half. I asked him to carry half, and I would carry the other half while he was deployed. Upon his return we would reunite the halves and have a party. When Nate returned safe and sound we did have a party but not using *that* hundred-dollar bill. I had each of the halves prepared so that they can be displayed. I have the half Nate carried through combat on my desk. He has the half that I carried with me. This constantly reminds us of the

Lord's faithfulness wherever Nate happened to be. God is with you everywhere.

HE REIGNS ALL THE TIME

Human sovereigns rule for a limited period of time. In the United States, for example, an individual can only hold the presidency for two terms. In some nations, leaders may rule a lot longer. For example, Queen Victoria reigned over the United Kingdom of Great Britain for sixty-four years. The Scriptures, however, teach us, "The LORD will reign forever and ever" (Exodus 15:18). It can't be put more plainly than that. There was never a time that he did not reign and there will never be a time when his reign comes to an end. "You, O LORD, are on high forever" (Psalm 92:8). He never needs to takes a nap, either! "He who watches over Israel will neither slumber nor sleep" (Psalm 121:4 NIV). The great result is that God is caring for us *all the time.* "It is in vain that you rise up early and go late to rest, eating the bread of anxious toil; for he gives to his beloved sleep" (Psalm 127:2). The message of the psalmist is that there is no need to stay up worrying or to lose sleep over things because the Lord is always watching out for us.

God is with you all the time, even though it might not always seem that way. There were many times in my wife Barb's life when she doubted whether the Lord was watching over her. When she was four years old, her father and mother had a nasty fight. Her dad stormed out the door in a rage. Within an hour there was a knock at the door. It was a policeman informing the family that her father had died in an accident with his motorcycle. Her mother never quite recovered from the loss, which manifested itself in mental instability. She married a man who couldn't hold a job and had been in and out of jail. She thought she could reform him. She was wrong. On several occasions he made inappropriate sexual advances to Barb and her sister. The situation became so serious that the courts intervened and removed them from danger. One aunt graciously took Barb in and another took in her sister. Barb's Aunt Mabel and Uncle Dave were very gracious and kind, treating her like their own daughter. But then Uncle Dave was diagnosed with cancer. He died after months of terrible suffering. Barb felt abandoned once again.

It was shortly after this that Barb recommitted her life to the Lord. It was then that she realized that despite her hardships and the absence of an earthly father, her heavenly Father was with her all along. Knowing that God is with her, that despite all of the hard things in life he was watching and keeping her, has changed the way she thinks about her past—and her future. Not that the sad things from her past have been instantly healed. But now she has a different way of thinking about her life because she knows her heavenly Father and knows that he intends everything ultimately for her good. She learned that he was with her all the time—even though it might not have seemed that way.

HE REIGNS OVER EVERYTHING

To affirm that God is sovereign is also to assert that he is in charge. He is in control. It is not sufficient merely to say that God reigns everywhere all the time. He reigns over *everything* and *everyone*. This is where it really gets personal. He is in charge of all of the circumstances of life.

My mother was a woman of faith. I remember listening to her talk in her later years about how age had given her a new sense of thanksgiving to the Lord. She would speak of how wonderful it was to look back on her life and see in retrospect how he had led her throughout her entire life. This is often how the Lord works. When we are in the middle of things, especially when life is difficult, we sometimes wonder whether the Lord is paying attention. His ways are often mysterious to us as we walk through hardship, but there is comfort in knowing that he is still at work in the midst of trials.

I have a friend with whom I attended seminary; upon graduation he became the minister of outreach at Coral Ridge Presbyterian Church in Fort Lauderdale. While serving there he made several close friends, including a couple named Jack and Lois. One year, Lois wanted to surprise her husband with a unique Christmas present. He had always wanted to go on a hot air balloon ride and she was determined to make it happen, but it was very expensive. Lois asked my friend if he would be willing to go along and share the surprise and the cost. After consulting with his wife, my friend concluded that the adventure was a little too expensive for them at the time so, with regrets, he declined the invitation. A few days before Christmas in 1979 the surprise was sprung, to Jack's delight, and he and two of his friends set out, along with the pilot.

Horrifyingly, the wicker gondola struck four power lines and turned into a fireball. The pilot was unable to land the balloon, and the fire caused the balloon to rise. With their families watching in disbelief as they followed by car, two of the passengers jumped from the flaming basket at 150 feet, and another at 1,500 feet. All aboard fell to their deaths.

It is difficult to imagine the heartbreak of the wives and children as they rushed to the lifeless bodies of their loved ones. Where did they find their comfort? First-responders reported being amazed as they came on the scene, listening to the tearful women comforting their children with the assurance that their loved ones were in heaven. Those dads and husbands were men of faith; they knew that, for the believer in Jesus, to be absent from the body is to be present with the Lord (2 Corinthians 5:8). Of course the families were devastated, but there was comfort in the knowledge that their husbands and dads were safely home with the Lord.

Another source of comfort might amaze you, but it speaks directly to how knowing God's reign helps our mindscape. My pastor friend and his wife visited Lois shortly after the accident. As they shed tears together, Lois turned and said, "I would have gone crazy had I not believed in the sovereignty of God."

What did she mean by this? From a human perspective she had arranged for the balloon ride. She had made all the arrangements not only for Jack, but also for his friends. She had chosen the day. Carrying this logic to its conclusion, she could have concluded that *she* was responsible for her husband's death. However, she was a woman of faith and understood that behind these events was the mystery of God's plan and providence. The answer to the "why did this happen?" question is hidden in the counsel of his will. However, the promise of God is clear.

"And we know that God causes all things to work together for good to those who love God, to those who are called according to His purpose" (Romans 8:28 NASB). Many who have written about this verse have rightly observed that the verse does not say that "all things are good"—because all things are *not* good. Death is not good. It is described as our enemy (1 Corinthians 15:58). In fact, my friend who lost her fourteen-year-old daughter came up with an accurate expression to describe death and its aftermath. She simply said, "This stinks." She is exactly right!

Many of the things we experience are terrible, but this is not the end of the story for those who trust in the Lord. Romans 8:28 teaches that all things "*work together* for good" (emphasis added). Yes, we grieve, but we grieve embracing the promise of life after death based on Jesus's resurrection from the dead. Yes, we suffer, but we suffer embracing our sovereign God in whose unsearchable wisdom we find comfort.

But how does this work out practically? How does meditating on whatever is noble help our mindscape when we're in the middle of hard times?

AN HONEST ADMISSION

The first thing you need to do is make a very fundamental admission: "God is God and I'm not." This is actually a great summary of the Bible's teaching. Every single day we live our lives in one of two ways: either I'm in charge or God is. How "large" is God in your mindscape? Is he in the foreground, prominent in your thoughts, or is he like a distant peak that is just *there*?

In the previous chapter, we mentioned that every human being is made in the image of God. One of the results of this is that we are always trying to exercise sovereignty. We try to create our little kingdoms over which we reign and have control. This might be at home, at work, or even when we get behind the steering wheels of our cars. We seek to assert our right to rule the highways with more pressure on the gas pedal or with the tap of the horn. "This lane is mine!" "You're driving too slowly!" Or we yell, "Hurry up and go!" when the light turns green. Unless you have humbled yourself and admitted that God is God and you're not, exercising your own sovereignty is the only resort left to you. However, any assertions that you're in control fall flat when things go wrong or when things don't turn out that way you expect. No, you are not a very effective god. And, although I try as well, I'm not either!

A COMFORTING POSITION

If you're willing to admit that the true God is God, you are now in a position to claim his promises and to know that in all things he is at work—even when you don't understand. When hardship comes you can respond with faith, not fear; peace instead of panic. The Scriptures are clear that the Lord uses trials to build our character and make us stronger. If we really believe this, James writes, it changes our attitude toward hardship. "Count it all joy, my brothers, when you meet trials of various kinds, for you know that the testing of your faith produces steadfastness. And let steadfastness have its full effect, that you may be perfect and complete, lacking in nothing" (James 1:2–4).

Joy? Are you serious? Yes—*if* you really believe that the Lord is at work behind the scenes for the good and that on the other side of the trials you will be stronger. The word translated "testing" is also used to describe the process of putting precious metals through fire, by which they were not only shown to be genuine but were purified. It was a test that expected a positive result. Remember, as Paul was writing the words we're focusing on from Philippians, he was in a Roman prison. But this letter is known as his most joyful letter! Even though Paul is behind bars, he urges his readers to rejoice. In all four chapters (a total of eight times) he calls upon them to rejoice together with him. "Finally, my brothers, rejoice in the Lord" (Philippians 3:1). He reminds them that joy should characterize their lives *all the time*. "Rejoice in the Lord *always*; again I will say, rejoice" (Philippians 4:4).

How could Paul be filled with such joy in these circumstances? He understood that the Lord was sovereignly guiding him as he sought to be a messenger of the gospel of Jesus Christ. He had adversaries who were trying to outshine him in ministry. What was Paul's response? "Only that in every way, whether in pretense or in truth, Christ is proclaimed, and in that I rejoice. Yes, and I will rejoice" (Philippians 1:18). What about the advance of his mission while stuck under Roman house arrest? "I want you to know, brothers, that what has happened to me has really served to advance the gospel, so that it has become known throughout the whole imperial guard and to all the rest that my imprisonment is for Christ" (Philippians 1:12–13). What about the prospect of losing his life in the process? "As it is my eager expectation and hope that I will not be at all ashamed, but that with full courage now as always Christ will be honored in my body, whether by life or by death. For to me to live is Christ, and to die is gain" (Philippians 1:20–21). He goes on to explain that if he is allowed to live he will continue to serve his Lord. If he dies, he will be with the Lord! This is what it looks like to trust in the Lord who reigns.

It would have been easy for Paul to have hung his head and had a personal pity party. Did you ever notice how helpful pity parties are? They are not very helpful at all. The only thing they accomplish is making you and everyone else around you miserable. Paul not only encourages the Philippians on what to include in their lives, by God's grace, but what to *remove*. From his jail cell he writes, "Do all things without grumbling or disputing" (Philippians 2:14 NASB). Though you will always find those who will join in when you grumble and complain, they accomplish nothing. Whining also represents a deficiency in our trust in the Lord who has promised to sovereignly care for us. Instead, turn to the Lord who rules all, looks after all, and pour out your heart to him. He hears your cries for mercy—and will answer when you call to him.

FROM MINDSCAPE TO LIFESCAPE

Paul gives us a very good example of how belief in the sovereign majestic God helps us. Remember that the word "noble" can be understood as "that which causes you to look up." Don't forget to "look up" to the Lord every day. When you do this, you rise above the discouraging dilemmas you face. It enables you to get the 50,000-foot view of life. Have you ever noticed how small and insignificant things look from the perspective of your seat in an airliner? The Lord is high and exalted. He knows where you are, what has been, and what is to come. He is guiding you and directing you as you seek to follow him.

Paul reminds his readers that "he who began a good work in you will bring it to completion at the day of Jesus Christ" (Philippians 1:6). Not only is the Lord not finished with you yet, but he always finishes what he starts!

Every day on my drive to work I pass a construction project that hasn't changed for the past few years. It is a rather large building, but there are only three walls and no roof. The elevator shaft is open to the elements and the whole site is now beginning to show evidence of deterioration. But this is not a picture of any one of us. Instead God is patiently at work, transforming all who have put their faith in Jesus. Aren't you glad that the Lord hasn't run out of the patience or the love to change your mindscape and lifescape to bring you to glory and fully conform you to the image of his Son one day? He will never give up on you!

How does the vista of God's noble sovereignty counter the worry weeds in your mindscape? What usually goes through your mind when you worry? Of what does worry fundamentally consist? Doesn't it consist largely of focusing on what *might* happen or what *could* go wrong? If the Lord is sovereign and has promised to work all things for good, there is no need to concern yourself. Be honest: How many times have the terrible things you imagined actually happened? Probably not very often. Embracing the sovereign rule of God over your life is a source of great comfort, joy, and security. There is no reason for despair. There is no point in being anxious. I would invite you to join the ranks of those of us who get up every morning and remind ourselves that we are *not* God. And then look up to the one true God of the universe, who controls all for our good and his glory. There is peace in remembering the truth that we are not sovereign but live and work under Someone else's rule. Because of my understanding of this truth, I like to call myself a "sovereigntist." Whatever word you use to describe yourself, I can assure you that peace is to be found in trusting the One who is truly majestic and reigns over all.

KEEP ON KEEPING ON

Whenever one speaks of the sovereignty of God it is important to be reminded of the Bible's emphasis on human responsibility. Being a "sovereigntist" is not to embrace a "let go and let God" attitude toward life but rather to live our lives in faith and obedience. Though Paul was completely secure in Christ and convinced of God's promise to bring him to his heavenly home, he was also convinced of his responsibility to follow in faith. After assuring the Philippians of their security in Christ, he reminds them to "work out your own salvation with fear and trembling, for it is God who works in you, both to will and to work for his good pleasure" (Philippians 2:12b–13).

Our salvation is a wonderful gift that is to be put to good use. We are called to yield to the Lord and walk in his ways through the power he provides. Paul describes his own attitude with the words of the runner moving toward the finish line. He uses the terms "press on to make it my own," "straining forward," and again "I press on toward the goal for the prize of the upward call of God in Christ Jesus" (Philippians 3:12–14).

The Bible teaches the truth of God's sovereignty *and* human responsibility. J.I. Packer reminds us, "C.H. Spurgeon was once asked if he could reconcile these two truths to each other. 'I wouldn't try,' he replied; 'I never reconcile friends.' Friends?— yes, friends. This is the point that we have to grasp. In the Bible, divine sovereignty and human responsibility are not enemies. They are not uneasy neighbors; they are not in an endless state of cold war with each other. They are friends, and they work together."[6]

The Lord is sovereign over your circumstances and, in Christ, is working all things (even bad things) for good. When your troubles, worries, and cares begin to clutter your mindscape, remind yourself of his majestic reign as he wisely directs circumstances to accomplish his purpose in and through you for his glory!

FOOD FOR THOUGHT

1. How does "whatever is noble" flow from "whatever is true?" How does it cause you to "look up"? List examples, if possible.

2. How much of a "sovereigntist" are you? In other words, how committed are you to living in the knowledge that "God is God and I'm not"? Where do you still have trouble doing this? Why?

3. Can you think of things in your life that were difficult at the time, but in retrospect you see the Lord's hand at work? How willing are you to believe that the same is true for the difficulties you face now?

4. What difference does it make to your mindscape if God's in charge rather than you? Use something you're dealing with now as a basis for your answer—no matter how well or badly you're doing with it right now.

MEMORY VERSE

Romans 8:28: "And we know that for those who love God all things work together for good, for those who are called according to his purpose."

5

Whatever Is Right

❦

He leads the humble in what is right, and teaches the humble his way.

Psalm 25:9

I hope you now see that the vistas of "whatever is true" and "whatever is noble" are foundational to your new mindscape. As Paul continues to guide us in what to think about when we're not worrying or praying he comes to "whatever is *right*." This leads to a very important question that everyone must answer: How do you decide what is right? I think you will agree that this is very closely related to the question "what is true?" discussed a couple of chapters earlier.

These days you hear a lot about the importance of having a moral compass. A moral compass is "anything which serves to guide a person's decisions based on morals or virtues."[1] The truth of the matter is that everyone *has* a moral compass—that is, a set of values and standards that guides their behavior. Yes, even you. Your moral compass may have been formed by family upbringing, culture, peers, or most likely a combination of them all. But anyone who has ever used a compass understands that unless the compass and map are properly oriented, you get lost very quickly.

One of the challenges in using a real compass is that there is a difference between magnetic north (that to which your compass points) and true north. This difference is called declination. The earth's magnetic field is always changing due to the instability of its molten core. The declination factor changes over time and from location to location on the surface of the earth. In fact, magnetic north is moving faster than ever, at roughly forty miles per year.[2] The magnetic field also seems to be weakening. Therefore, even when one has a compass, it is possible to be off track.

How does one find true *moral* north? How do people decide what is right? There are certainly factors that move people away from true north. It seems that movement from true *moral* north is happening faster, and going farther, than even true *magnetic* north! Increasingly, "right" is determined by majority vote. Whatever the most people think is right is embraced as moral. This is called consensus morality, and it is very risky business. Imagine that you're on a hike with a group of people, and as the sun is beginning to set you come to a fork in the road. One path leads to the head of the trail and the way home. The other path leads deeper into the dark forest. There is indecision in the group as to which way to go. Someone has a compass that indicates the correct path. However, there is another traveler who doubts the compass and urges people to go the other (wrong) way. The group heads off into the woods and will spend an unexpected long dark cold night.

Likewise, consensus morality leads to darkness and confusion. Think about how this plays out in our world. As the consensus in our culture about right and wrong has shifted away from the biblical standards, life *has* gotten darker and more confusing. The proliferation of pornography use, the rise in premarital sex, and the many marriages broken by infidelity have far-reaching negative consequences. Far from being harmless choices, the individuals and families I counsel have sadly described to me the relational destruction that accompanies moral decisions that are reduced to what "feels right" at the time.

If there *is* a true moral north, where is it to be found? The word Paul uses for "right" can also be translated "righteous." What comes to mind first of all when we hear this word is the complete moral perfection of God. "The LORD is righteous in all his ways and kind in all his works" (Psalm 145:17). "Gracious is the LORD, and righteous; our God is merciful" (Psalm 116:5). Righteousness is one of God's fundamental attributes. It also describes what he *does*. "The King in his might loves justice. You have established equity; you have executed justice and righteousness in Jacob" (Psalm 99:4). Gordon Fee helps us understand how Paul makes the connection. "As with truth, what is 'right' is always defined by God and his character. Thus, even though this is one of the cardinal virtues of Greek antiquity, in Paul it carries the further sense of 'righteousness,' so that it is not defined by merely human understanding of what is 'right' or 'just' but by God and his relationship with his people."[3]

The good news is that the God who is *righteous* has also revealed what is *right*. Even as he has revealed what is true, so he has applied truth to human behavior to enable us to know the right way. Even as truth is found in his inspired Word, so do we find what is right. "Righteous are you, O LORD, and right are your rules" (Psalm 119:137). "This God—his way is perfect; the word of the LORD proves true; he is a shield for all those who take refuge in him" (Psalm 18:30). These verses show the connection between his righteous character and what he reveals in the Scriptures. His will for us is revealed in his Word. The gift of the law to the Israelites in the wilderness was designed to provide direction on how to love God and one another. His top ten list found in the Ten Commandments begins with the *right* way to love God followed by the *right* way to love one another. Remember these commandments?

1. You shall have no other gods before me.
2. You shall not make for yourself an idol in the form of anything in heaven above, or on the earth beneath, or in the waters below.
3. You shall not misuse the name of the LORD your God.
4. Remember the Sabbath day by keeping it holy.
5. Honor your father and your mother, so that you may live long in the land the LORD your God is giving you.

6. You shall not murder.
7. You shall not commit adultery.
8. You shall not steal.
9. You shall not give false testimony against your neighbor.
10. You shall not covet (abridged from Exodus 20:1–17; cf. Deuteronomy 5:7–21).

These verses *are* true moral north. They are all about the right way to love God with all your heart, soul, and mind and your neighbor as yourself. They tell you the right way to think about 1) and 2) God's place in your life; 3) God's place in your speech; 4) the Sabbath day; 5) your parents and authority; 6) the sanctity of life; 7) the sanctity of marriage; 8) the sanctity of private property; 9) the sanctity of truth; and 10) the need to guard one's heart.

However, it is important to understand that these cannot be boiled down merely to a checklist of behaviors. There have always been people who have sought to see the Ten Commandments as boxes to be checked to punch one's ticket to heaven. In the days of Jesus, the Pharisees were such people. They thought they had it all figured out, but Jesus reminded them that these commandments were more than superficial behaviors. In the Sermon on the Mount he spoke these words:

> You have heard that it was said to those of old, "*You shall not murder*; and whoever murders will be liable to judgment." But I say to you that everyone who is angry with his brother will be liable to judgment; whoever insults his brother

will be liable to the council; and whoever says, "You fool!" will be liable to the hell of fire. So if you are offering your gift at the altar and there remember that your brother has something against you, leave your gift there before the altar and go. First be reconciled to your brother, and then come and offer your gift. Come to terms quickly with your accuser while you are going with him to court, lest your accuser hand you over to the judge, and the judge to the guard, and you be put in prison. Truly, I say to you, you will never get out until you have paid the last penny.

You have heard that it was said, *"You shall not commit adultery."* But I say to you that everyone who looks at a woman with lustful intent has already committed adultery with her in his heart. (Matthew 5:21–28, emphasis added)

In these and the surrounding verses Jesus is showing the bankruptcy and danger of merely having a skin-deep view of what's right. The Lord is concerned about the heart. Most of us can "check" the box that we never took someone's life. Before you start feeling too good about yourself, though, Jesus adds that this commandment also includes our heart attitude toward other people. You might not kill someone with your hand, but have you harbored unrighteous anger in your mind and expressed it in your words? Jesus says, "Guilty!"

Jesus goes on to address another commandment on God's top-ten list, the one about faithfulness in marriage. His application focuses on husbands. So you never cheated on your wife? Really? Maybe you never literally hopped into bed with your neighbor's wife, but what about in your mind? Jesus goes deeper. Have you ever had an impure desire for a woman ever in your life? Be honest. Jesus says, "Guilty!" because whatever is right goes deeper than mere external behavior.

On a separate occasion, the adversaries of Jesus tried to trip him up with this question.

"Teacher, which is the great commandment in the Law?" (Matthew 22:36). The questioner probably imagined that it would take some nerve to put one commandment above another, but I think you'll agree that it's still a very good question. If you boil everything down, what's most important? Jesus replied: "'You shall love the Lord your God with all your heart and with all your soul and with all your mind.' This is the great and first commandment" (22:37–38). There you have it. Jesus reinforced the same order as in the top ten of Exodus 20: Put God first. But he didn't stop there: "And a second is like it: 'You shall love your neighbor as yourself'" (22:39).

Let me take a moment here to express something that's really bugged me about how some preachers have interpreted this verse; in fact, I heard it again from a TV preacher just the other day. They interpret it like this: "What this verse teaches is that in order to love others we need to have a healthy self-image, lots of love for oneself. So, I need to work on loving myself more." But notice that the words of Jesus presume and understand that I *already* love myself plenty. In fact, as we saw earlier, if it were up to me I would rule the world and have everyone bow down to me.

Jesus is in fact encouraging us to bring our treatment of others *up* to the way we treat ourselves; to think as highly of others as we think of ourselves; to give other folks the "breaks" we give to ourselves. Isn't this the very heart of what has come to be known as the Golden Rule: "So whatever you wish that others would do to you, do also to them" (Matthew 7:12)? Note that the greatest commandment emphasizes the priority of our putting the Lord first and that the second-greatest focuses on our loving other people. This is the order of priority that we see in the Ten Commandments as well. In fact, after Jesus concludes his statement of the two greatest commandments he says, "On these two commandments depend all the Law and the Prophets" (Matthew 22:40).

Both of these commandments bring us to the same conclusion that Jesus brings us to at the end of the Sermon on the Mount: We are unable to attain this standard of righteousness. As we asked in an earlier chapter, whom do you know that loves the Lord with all his heart and with all his soul and with all his mind all the time? No one that I know. Whom do you know whose love for other people rises to the level of his love for himself? None of the people I know do.

All doubts are removed about what Jesus is getting at when you look at how he states the ultimate true moral north for mankind. "You therefore must be perfect, as your heavenly Father is perfect" (Matthew 5:48). This leads us to the place to which Jesus wants us to come—to the end of ourselves and our own sense of self-righteousness. The whole class has failed. We have a problem in thinking about "whatever is right." We do not focus on true moral north but tend to drift with the magnetic north of our own making. Here's an example of how American culture has drifted from true moral north. A couple of decades ago, two researchers determined to put their research to the pulse of American morality. "For one day in their lives, more than 2,000 Americans were given the opportunity to express what they believed about the things that really matter. Each of them answered over 1,800 questions."[4] They asked about everything! Of interest to our discussion of "whatever is right" is the American view of true moral north. "Only 13 percent of us believe in all Ten Commandments. Forty percent of us believe in five of the Ten Commandments."[5] Here's how respondents related to some of the individual commandments:

1. I will steal from those who won't really miss it (74 percent).
2. I will lie when it suits me so long as it doesn't cause any real damage (64 percent).
3. I will cheat on my spouse—after all, given the chance, he or she will do the same (53 percent).[6]

It absolutely boggles the mind to think about how far culture has drifted from God's true moral north. Of course all humans all the time are drifting from the true north of God's morality. But at least there used to be more agreement with God's moral north! The natural question that comes to mind is "How do people decide what is right? How do they decide what to do?" Patterson and Kim revealed that "Americans are making up their own rules, their own laws. In effect, we are all making up our own moral codes."[7]

This is reinforced by two more recent national surveys conducted by Barna Research that I cited earlier, one among adults and one among teenagers. Both groups were asked if they believed that there were moral absolutes that are unchanging or whether moral truth is relative to the circumstances. By a nearly three-to-one margin (sixty-four percent to twenty-two percent), adults said truth is always relative to the person and their situation. The perspective was even more lopsided among teenagers, eighty-three percent of whom said moral truth depends on the circumstances, and only six percent of whom said moral truth is absolute.[8] What most people are saying, therefore, is that there is no such thing as true moral north. If that's the case, how do they decide what's right?

By far the most common basis for moral decision-making was doing whatever felt right or comfortable in a situation. Nearly four out of ten teenagers and more than three out of ten adults described this as their primary consideration.[9]

I hope you can see that such a perspective will lead to chaos in society as everyone decides what is right for himself. If you take a look at the book of Judges, you see some of the most horrific examples of what people can do to one another. It is increasingly becoming like it was in those shocking days: "In those days there was no king in Israel. Everyone did what was right in his own eyes" (Judges 21:25). Take a moment and ask *yourself* these questions:

- How do I decide what is right?
- Am I making up my own rules?
- How would I respond when asked about the Ten Commandments?

The challenge in considering "whatever is right" is to recognize that our natural mindscape—the one with which we are born—is not inclined to true moral north. We are not inclined to righteousness but to unrighteousness. "As it is written: 'None is righteous, no, not one; no one understands; no one seeks for God. All have turned aside; together they have become worthless; no one does good, not even one'" (Romans 3:10–12). If you think you're not that bad, remember the Sermon on the Mount and the greatest commandments. Is there any hope to be properly oriented to true moral north?

You might be wondering what all of this has to do with worry. There are at least two ways that being confused about what is right and not having a true moral north will bring fear and anxiety into your life. First, although you might think you already know what is right—God has given you a conscience. We all have a sense of right and wrong, even if it is imperfect. So when we drift away from the true moral north, guilt comes with it. We have an uneasy sense that something is wrong. We might try to talk ourselves out of it, but the sense that things are not right stays with us as a cloud over our minds. Second, without a true moral compass, chaos does happen in our lives. When we fail to love God and others—the consequences are broken relationships and bad choices that have bad consequences—

we have all seen and probably experienced those. The anxiety and fear that accompany those bad choices can be overwhelming. But how do we escape the cycle of guilt and the brokenness that comes with it?

Earlier in this book we talked about pushing the reset button. There was only one person who was perfectly righteous and who *always* did whatever was right. That person was Jesus Christ. He perfectly kept the law. He was perfectly righteous. You want to see what the perfect love of God looks like? Look at Jesus. You want to see what the perfect love of people looks like? Look at Jesus.

However, Jesus didn't come to be a mere example of what is right so we can just "be like Jesus" and everything will fall into place. No, he came to do something about our unrighteousness and thus change our fundamental orientation to "whatever is right." In a remarkable act of compassion, "He made Him who knew no sin to be sin on our behalf, so that we might become the righteousness of God in Him" (2 Corinthians 5:21 NASB). This is the most amazing transaction in all of history. My sin was placed on him, so that his righteousness can be mine. My unrighteousness was exchanged for his righteousness. Amazing grace! Notice that Paul says that the result is that "we might become the righteousness of God *in Him*." Not only are our sins forgiven, but now we stand before God as righteous because the righteousness of Jesus has become ours. Our guilt is gone. Our fears are stilled. Our brokenness is redeemed. Theologians refer to this as the doctrine of imputation. John Murray has described the transaction this way:

The one ground upon which the imputation of the righteousness of Christ is ours is the union with Christ. In other words, the justified person is constituted righteous by the obedience of Christ because of the solidarity established between Christ and the justified person. The solidarity constitutes the bond by which the righteousness of Christ becomes that of the believer.[10]

This righteousness we have before God is ours not because of our performance, but because of the perfect obedience of Jesus Christ placed to our account. This becomes ours through faith. As Paul wrote, "Therefore, since we have been justified by faith, we have peace with God through our Lord Jesus Christ" (Romans 5:1).

The Scriptures are clear that this right standing (justification) before God, which can never change, leads to a new mindscape (peace with God) and a new way of living (sanctification) in which we grow throughout the rest of our lives. You have now been oriented to the true moral north. You have been given the gift of the Holy Spirit to assist you in experiencing the transformation from the old mindscape to the new mindscape, especially in understanding and doing whatever is right. Paul shows us what this difference looks like:

For those who live according to the flesh set their *minds* on the things of the flesh, but those who live according to the Spirit set their *minds* on the things of the Spirit. For to set the *mind* on the flesh is death, but to set the *mind* on the

Spirit is life and peace. For the *mind* that is set on the flesh is hostile to God, for it does not submit to God's law; indeed, it cannot. Those who are in the flesh cannot please God. You, however, are not in the flesh but in the Spirit, if in fact the Spirit of God dwells in you. (Romans 8:5–9, emphasis added)

Through Jesus we are given the gift of the Spirit, in order that we might set our minds not on the flesh (the old mindscape) but on the things of the Spirit, which are identified in this text as God's law. This is truly liberating! We are no longer in bondage to the old self-focused idea of what is right, but instead have a new understanding and a new desire to know whatever is right and to see its fruit in our lives. Whatever is right is no longer defined by me, myself, and I (or the culture) but by the Word of God. There is peace in knowing we don't have to decide ourselves on the right way to love God and others. We can trust that God's Word will guide and help us. There is peace in knowing that our sins are forgiven. And that when we turn away from our true moral north, as soon as we notice we are drifting, we can go to Jesus for forgiveness and ask the Spirit to help us and change us. This is a life where anxieties are stilled—we are guided by the Spirit and forgiven when we fail.

"WHATEVER IS RIGHT" IN A WORLD OF WRONG

If "whatever is right" is a rare commodity in the world in which we live—and in our own hearts, for that matter—how are we to go about developing this particular vista of our mindscape? How can we reduce the worries that come from confusion in orientation to keeping our eyes on true moral north on a daily basis? Here are just a few practical suggestions to get you started:

1. Meditate on what you know to be right. Again, this is similar to the development of the vista of truth. Ground your heart and mind in the Word of God so that you become increasingly focused on what is right and sharpened in discerning what it looks like. In speaking of "going deep" into the Scriptures, the writer to the Hebrews says, "But solid food is for the mature, for those who have their powers of discernment trained by constant practice to distinguish good from evil" (Hebrews 5:14). If you pay attention to television, movies, and advertising, there is a lot of wrong being highlighted and endorsed. Saturating yourself in the Scriptures will help you see the difference.

2. Do what you know is right. This vista of your mindscape definitely has an impact on your lifescape. Knowing what is right is half the battle. Doing it is the far more difficult half.

There are times that we know what is right but we do not do it. There are different reasons for this. Sometimes we're afraid of what other people will think. Other times doing what is right will cost us money, time, or relationships. Paying *all* your taxes costs you money. Obeying the speed limit costs you time. Loving your enemy may cost you friends. The truth is that we cannot do what is right in our own strength any more than we can save ourselves by our own strength. The Spirit not only shows you what is right, but will help you get there.

There is a story told about a traveler who got lost in a rural farming region (before the days of GPS). He stopped to ask directions of a farmer who clearly knew the territory. The farmer began to blurt out complicated directions, "Go to the end of this field and turn left. Then continue until you come to a broken water pump and the end of a tree-lined lane...." The farmer stopped in the middle of his sentence and said, "How about if I just hop in? I'm headed that way anyhow." Likewise, you and I have the presence of the Spirit in our lives to show us what is right, and he empowers us to get there! "But I say, walk by the Spirit, and you will not gratify the desires of the flesh" (Galatians 5:16). To "walk by the Spirit" implies walking not only in the wisdom and direction he provides but also through his power. This requires a conscious determination to experience this transformation.

Don't be discouraged. Growth in "whatever is right" is a process. Sometimes it is "three steps forward and two steps back." Sometimes it is "two steps forward and *three* steps back"! Do not give up because the Lord will never give up on you. Along the way he will show you and empower you to know and to do "whatever is right."

3. *"Whatever is right" and worry.* How does thinking about and doing "whatever is right" impact your worry weeds? First of all, lots of our worries arise from not knowing *what to do.* Having your heart and mind sharpened on the knowledge of what is right will help you know what, and what not, to do. If you know what is right and act upon it, you will have a clear (peaceful) conscience.

You might be in a situation at work where your boss asks you to do something unethical. You know what is right, and so you must decline and ask the Lord to give you the wisdom to provide an ethical alternative. Doing what is right, applying truth to life is what the bible calls "wisdom." When in doubt, always do what is right. If there is going to be trouble, make sure that the trouble comes from doing the right thing rather than what is wrong. "Now who is there to harm you if you are zealous for what is good? But even if you should suffer for righteousness' sake, you will be blessed. Have no fear of them, nor be troubled" (1 Peter 3:13–14). To do what is right is to align yourself with the God of righteousness. As Paul wrote, "If God is for us, who can be against us?" (Romans 8:31). The answer is obvious: *No one!* When you are aligned with what is right in the eyes of the Lord, you have no need to worry.

FOOD FOR THOUGHT

1. Why is "whatever is right" an important vista in your mindscape? How, in your own words, is it related to "whatever is true?"

2. From what sources do you get your understanding of what's right? How reliable are those sources? Why do you say that?

3. Reflect again on the Ten Commandments and on Jesus's words about them in the Sermon on the Mount (pages 36–37. Based on what Jesus says, how well do you obey the Ten Commandments—*really*?

4. Do you agree that you *can't* keep the law? Why or why not?

5. How can truly believing that Jesus came to "become sin for you that you might become the righteousness of God in him" alter your mindscape and affect your ability to live in a way that pleases God?

6. How does growing in "whatever is right" help you with your worry weeds? How can meditating on "whatever is right" help you right now? Be specific, in both cases.

MEMORY VERSES

Matthew 22:37-40: "You shall love the Lord your God with all your heart and with all your soul and with all your mind. This is the great and first commandment. And a second is like it: You shall love your neighbor as yourself. On these two commandments depend all the Law and the Prophets."

Also, if you've never memorized the Ten Commandments, it would be a very good exercise. Review, and internalize, the list on pages 70–71.

6

Whatever Is Pure

❦

Blessed are the pure in heart, for they shall see God.
Matthew 5:8

One of my favorite TV shows is *America's Funniest Home Videos,* and from time to time there is a clip where someone is trying to get into a boat with one foot on the dock and one foot in the boat. What happens? If a decisive choice between the dock and the boat is not made the person winds up neither on the dock nor in the boat but in the water! Of course everyone laughs while the hapless person who tried to keep one foot on land and one foot on the boat is soaking wet. This is a great picture of what happens to us spiritually when we have a divided heart instead of a pure heart. Thinking about "whatever is pure" is the how the Spirit helps us keep our lives and hearts stable and firm.

I hope, as we've worked our way through these vistas of the new mindscape, that you've been able to see the inspired progression. The vista of truth is the foundation of everything. If you haven't settled the question of the source of truth in your life, I'm afraid you're set up for a very troubled mindscape. Next came "whatever is noble," in which we looked at the sovereign majesty of the Lord over all and the comfort that knowledge brings, particularly when times are tough. "Whatever is right" came next, and with that our vistas became even more practical. Where is true moral north to be found? We argued that it is found in the Lord's revelation of the Scriptures. Asking for the Spirit to help us focus on each of these vistas in the details of our lives is a very practical way that God has given us to combat the anxieties and worries that fill our minds.

Paul then gives us yet another vista upon which we can focus, to comfort, encourage, and bring the peace of Christ to our hearts—whatever is *pure*.

A PURE HEART

In describing the term, Richard Trench notes that it "signifies often the pure in the highest sense."[1] You can see why the concept of "holiness" is so closely related to the concept of purity. It was not merely an abstract concept, either. It came to have very practical implications for all of life. Gordon Fee observes, "Thus 'whatever things are pure' has to do with whatever is not 'besmirched' or 'tainted' in some way by evil."[2]

We've got to begin by acknowledging once again that the human heart and mind isn't very pure. Let's be honest. Purity isn't something that you hear a lot about these days. What comes to mind for many when they hear the word "pure" is Ivory Soap, which was touted as being 99$^{44/100}$ percent pure. Even that reference might be unknown to younger readers. While—or rather, because—we hear so little about purity these days, developing this vista is one of the most challenging of all. But, like all of the vistas that Paul mentions in Philippians 4, failure to develop it can be a source of serious trouble and anxiety. Why is this so?

Let's answer that question by looking at what it means to be "pure in heart." When Jesus said, "Blessed are the pure in heart for they will see God" as he preached the Sermon on the Mount, many of the huge crowd that had gathered to listen to his teaching understood what it meant to be *ceremonially* pure when it came to sacred celebrations and sacrifices. This is certainly what the religious leaders—the Scribes and Pharisees—thought about. They had the sacrifices, rites, and ceremonies of Judaism down to a science. Ceremonial purity *was* an important part of preparation to draw near to God. Everyone and everything that came near to God had to be purified and cleansed because the Lord himself is perfectly pure.

While these were important as pictures and signs of purity, they weren't the heart of the matter. Jesus was always pressing below the surface to challenge motives and one's true heart condition. The word used for "pure" by Jesus is the word from which we get our word "catharsis." In medical usage, a catharsis is something that cleanses the body. In psychiatric terms, a catharsis is an experience that purges or transforms. The goal of both is wholeness and health. So when Jesus spoke about being pure in heart, he meant that God is expecting *wholehearted* love toward him and others.

The idea of purity of heart meaning wholehearted love is not a new one. Remember that in the Old Testament, the Lord spoke through Moses saying, "You shall love the Lord your God with *all* your heart and with *all* your soul and with *all* your might" (Deuteronomy 6:5, emphasis added). Jesus later identified this as the Great Commandment (Mark 12:30). Similarly the prophet Hosea wrote, "For I desire steadfast love and not sacrifice, the knowledge of God rather than burnt offerings" (Hosea 6:6). Even (especially!) religious exercises must be accompanied by a heart turned toward the Lord. The prophet Isaiah expressed the Lord's complaint that "this people draw near with their mouth and honor me with their lips, while their hearts are far from me, and their fear of me is a commandment taught by men" (Isaiah 29:13). There was a disconnect between their hearts and what they said and did.

So purity of heart is wholehearted devotion to the Lord. One commentator wrote that to be pure in heart is to be "single-minded, *free from the tyranny of a divided self* which does not try to serve God and the world at the same time"[3] (emphasis added). That is the problem: "the tyranny of a divided self." There are all kinds of troublesome weeds in this family: hypocrisy, duplicity, two-facedness, and inconsistency, just to name a few. None of them are good. They are all hard to root out. Hypocrisy is probably the definitive antonym of purity of heart. This was the primary complaint of Jesus against the religious leaders of the day.

In fact, three times in the Sermon on the Mount (Matthew 6:2, 5, 16) Jesus tells the people *not* to be like the religious leaders because they only do what's "right" so people will see and praise them, and they only pray and fast to be heard and seen by others and not by God. In each case he refers to them as "hypocrites." This is an interesting word, too. It finds its source in the Greek theater where "hypocrite" was the word for an "actor." Actors in those days wore painted masks instead of makeup. Do you see the connection? A hypocrite is someone who is putting on a mask to play a role that is not who he really is. A hypocrite is pretending to be something that he really isn't. This was the problem Jesus had with the religious leaders; what you saw was *not* what you got! Especially since their mask was one of "painted on" religion. This was so serious that later in Matthew's gospel Jesus expressed seven "woes" against them. A "woe" was a warning of judgment upon them and was about the worst thing he could say to someone.

But before we start wagging a finger at these characters, let's admit that there is plenty of hypocrisy and duplicity in each one of us. Why do we live like this? The same reason the self-righteous leaders did. Because we want people to think well of us. We want them to think that we have it together. We want people to think we are good people. We want them to think we are nice people. We don't want people to know what we are really like or what we really think. We don't want them to know that while we are being very polite on the outside, on the inside we are seething with jealousy or anger. The bottom line is that we are trying to lift ourselves up (dare

I say idolizing ourselves?). We idolize our own reputation, our own pleasure, our own world.

Why does this kind of life produce stress and worry? Because there is always tension between the real you and the fake you. In your own heart you are wondering "who is the real me?" Are you the one who claims to know God and goes to church every Sunday? Or are you the person who harbors hate toward your "friend" or who can't free your mind from lust? Are you the person who claims to love your neighbors or the one who tries to avoid them when you see them at the store? The problem is that not only do you stress about who the real you is, but so do your family members and friends. This kind of duplicity is difficult to hide for very long in any relationship. "A hypocrite *says* one thing but *means* something else. He *pretends* to do one thing but *intends* to do another. He is play-acting, dissembling. He is hiding his real face under a mask"[4] (emphasis added). How can you really love someone and act this way toward them? This is stressful because it is a difficult balance to maintain.

The idea of "balance" is the perfect place to return to the earlier picture of one foot in the boat and one on the dock. If a decisive choice between the dock and the boat is not made, the person winds up neither on the dock nor in the boat but in the water! Purity of heart must begin with a decisive choice. You can't have one foot on the dock of commitment to the Lord and the other one in the moving boat of self-promotion. You will end up in the water. You can't have one foot on the dock of commitment to the Lord and the other foot in the boat of advancing your own fortune or reputation.

You will be all wet before you know it. James could not have put it any better when he wrote, "Draw near to God and he will draw near to you. Cleanse your hands, you sinners, and purify your hearts you double-minded" (James 4:8). This is easier said than done. But before we look at some steps to a pure mindscape, let's look at one specific example of a divided mind and heart.

A SERIOUS CHALLENGE
TO A PURE MIND

If you think about it, it makes sense that the world we live in sets the stage for a divided heart and divided life. The Bible teaches us that the world we live in is under the control of the evil one, and as we live here we will always be tempted to have a divided heart and mind. An area in which integrity of heart and mind is constantly challenged is in the area of sexual purity. A true enemy of the pure mind is our sex-obsessed culture that throws dirt at us 24/7 from every angle. You can't even settle down for an hour or two of television viewing without being challenged. A biennial report of the Kaiser Family Foundation revealed an alarming increase in the amount of sexual content on television. The study found that seventy percent of all shows include some sexual content and that these shows average five sexual scenes per hour, compared to fifty-six percent/3.2 scenes per hour in 1998 and sixty-four percent/4.4 scenes per hour in 2002.[5] As if that's not bad enough, you and your family can't escape during commercials either. According to one study, roughly one-fifth of all advertising uses overt sexual content to sell a product.[6]

Add to this the increasing number of pharmaceutical ads that address various forms of sexual dysfunction. It is quite challenging to have to explain to prepubescent children what's going on in these commercials.

"So what?" you might ask. As we've already seen, what we think about impacts our behavior. Have you become a little too comfortable with what the culture is dishing out? Have you become too permissive in what you allow your family to view? Don't deceive yourself into thinking that you just need to protect the children. This is having a negative impact on *your* mindscape, too.

As if the influence of popular media isn't enough, now there is the Internet with even greater opportunity to darken one's mindscape via easy access to pornography. "Pornography is everywhere, and the ease of a person being able to get their hands on it is turning countless numbers of people into porn addicts, becoming hooked without even knowing it."[7]

Trying to keep one foot in the boat of pornography with the other on the dock of commitment to the Lord and to your spouse is an unstable stance that will bring anxiety to your life and instability in your marriage. If you continue trying to maintain this divided life you will end up in choppy waters.

Its pernicious presence and practice are growing at a viral pace. The Internet also provides opportunity for "acting out" with real partners other than one's spouse. Everyone knows someone these days who "met someone on the Internet" whom they found more interesting than their own spouse. What does the Lord think about this? "Let marriage be held in honor among all, and let the marriage bed be undefiled, for God will judge the sexually immoral and adulterous" (Hebrews 13:4). As you can see, this is not harmless adult entertainment as some would like us to believe, but a real, measurable, and undeniable threat to individuals, families, and society—against which you must guard your mind.

Take a moment to think about how living a divided life in the area of sexual purity fills your mindscape with anxiety. Putting sexual lust first in your life—ahead of your relationship with God and your spouse—might feel exciting and pleasurable. But what is the end result? Your relationship with God and your spouse is ultimately damaged. If you are single, your ability to form an honest relationship with someone is seriously impacted. Ultimately, living a life of counterfeit relationships where we are at the center brings fear and anxiety. You worry if you will get caught. You worry about whether you can ever stop. You worry about your relationships. You worry about who you really are. Are you truly a follower of the Lord or are you a pretender? There's no doubt that there is self-deception at work.

Maybe your struggle is not with sexual issues. There might be other disconnects in your life between what you want to do and the way God is calling you to live. Whatever your particular struggle, the result will be a divided mind. When you think about what you want more than God, can you see how worry and fear come right along with what you desire? Contrast the way you are living with these words from the prophet Isaiah, "You keep him in perfect peace whose mind is stayed on you, because he trusts in you" (Isaiah 26:3). Perfect peace is a result of having a pure heart. And there is hope to all who are willing to look to the Lord for a pure heart and mind.

STEPS TO A PURE MINDSCAPE

1. First things first.

The first step goes back to where we have looked before; the natural human condition. When Jesus said, "Blessed are the pure in heart, for they shall see God" (Matthew 5:8), he was reminding us that what matters most is our internal disposition of heart and mind. The problem is: This is not our natural condition. We don't start out with pure minds.

In his anguish Job asked the question, "Can mortal man be in the right before God? Can a man be pure before his Maker?" (Job 4:17); he raises the question again: "What is man, that he can be pure? Or he who is born of woman, that he can be righteous?" (Job 15:14). And again. "How then can man be in the right before God? How can he who is born of woman be pure?" (Job 25:4). The same question is posed by wise King Solomon, "Who can say, 'I have made my heart pure; I am clean from my sin?'" (Proverbs 20:9).

The answer to all these questions is obvious: We cannot be pure in and of ourselves.

As we saw in our previous chapter, we have no righteousness of our own. By the same token, we have no purity of our own. This too is a gift of God through faith in Jesus Christ. We have a "positional purity" in union with him, and through that we have the opportunity to walk in his strength and experience increasing purity and holiness every day through his Holy Spirit who indwells us. Living out our union with Christ enables us to close the hypocrisy gap (the difference between what we should be and what we really are) and grow in integrity (consistency between who we are and who we are to become in Christ). Double-mindedness, duplicity, and self-deception become less present and less powerful. Wholeness in your relationships with God and with others becomes genuine.

In Psalm 24, David identifies the characteristics of those who can approach the holy God. The answer? "He who has clean hands and a pure heart, who does not lift up his soul to what is false and does not swear deceitfully. He will receive blessing from the LORD and righteousness from the God of his salvation" (Psalm 24:4–5). Notice his linking of purity of heart and deceiving others. They do not belong together. Rather, in the Lord, we have an increasing love for what is pure and a growing disdain for those things that corrupt our spirits and create the stress of being double-minded.

2. Be honest with yourself.

One day a little boy decided to call his Dad at work. When the Dad answered, the little boy asked, "Who is this?" Dad, recognizing his son's voice said, "The smartest man in the world." The little boy said, "I'm sorry. I must have a wrong number!" The honesty of children can sometimes be surprising, but it is usually quite refreshing, too. We need to be surprisingly and refreshingly honest with ourselves about what's settled into our thinking. Take an *honest* look at some of the duplicity that you are practicing in your life. Integrity is related to the word "integer." An integer is a whole number. Is your devotion to the Lord wholehearted? This goes a long way to determine whether or not you are a whole person, a person of integrity. Or are you living a fractured life as you are drawn to idolize the counterfeits this world has to offer including its big three: money, sex, or power. Be honest with yourself: Are there things in your mindscape of which you are ashamed for anyone else to see? Do you have a dirty mind? And did I just offend you? Let me put it a different way then: Do you have a pure mind? Are there thoughts and imaginations with which you have become comfortable but with which you shouldn't be comfortable, which are not consistent with your faith?

The problem with rotting things, whether they be jealousy, greed, or any other snare, is that they don't just sit there—they keep rotting and then begin to affect the things around them. Before you know it, your whole mindscape develops a certain stench about it. A high school friend of mine played the euphonium. It looks like a small tuba. We began to notice a very pungent smell coming from inside the instrument. He cleaned it out and found a small corn plant inside that had grown and then began to die and rot. It turns out that during a parade someone in the crowd had thrown one kernel of corn into his instrument. It only took that one small kernel to grow into a stinking distraction.

Do an honest assessment of the purity of your mindscape, and identify the foul things you've allowed in. It is something to which we must set our minds. In one of his sermons, Jonathan Edwards makes it clear that this is our responsibility to pursue:

> We must not think to excuse ourselves by saying that it is God's work, that we cannot purify our own hearts; for though it be God's work in one sense, yet it is equally our work in another; James 4:8, "Cleanse your hands ye sinners; and purify your hearts ye double-minded." If you do not engage in this work yourselves, and purify your own hearts, they will never be pure.[8]

Have you settled? Have you capitulated to an inappropriate state of mind? If you can honestly say that you are not willing to settle, then it is time to take a stand. Get both feet on solid ground.

3. Take your stand against impurity.

It's one thing to acknowledge the duplicity and self-deception you have allowed to become at home in your mind. It's another to clean house and to prevent the arrival of more. The process toward purity is like a battle. That old sinful nature still clings to us and those natural desires that are all too eager to return to old patterns. In C.S. Lewis's *Screwtape Letters*, the senior demon Screwtape gives his aspiring demon nephew Wormwood the following advice, "All that we can do is to encourage the humans to take the pleasures our Enemy [God] has produced, but at times and in ways that He has forbidden."[9] The distortion of natural desire is where impurity often begins. Given what we've already seen about the media and pornography, you know that you need to protect your input. This is an important way to protect the vista of purity in your mindscape.

Perhaps a good way to get a handle on the process of purity is to be reminded of the warning James provides as he describes the process of sin. "Each one is tempted when, by his own evil desire, he is dragged away and enticed. Then, after desire has conceived, it gives birth to sin; and sin, when it is full-grown, gives birth to death" (James 1:14–15 NIV 1984). Not too long ago, I heard a wonderful sermon by Derek Thomas in which he presented an exposition of the "armor of God" from the sixth chapter of Ephesians. He was talking about the importance of taking a stand against the evil one. As he discussed the traps that can be set by our sinful desires he noted that this becomes particularly dangerous when "desire meets opportunity."[10]

It is one thing to entertain impure thoughts in one's mind, but when the opportunity to "act out" presents itself, disaster is at hand. What becomes of the man who has fantasized about his coworker or neighbor and then suddenly finds himself alone with her? Desire has met opportunity and an appropriate outcome is in doubt. You know what I'm talking about. What if the situation about which you have fantasized actually presents itself? Would you be able to respond purely if your mind was already rehearsing impurity? Jonathan Edwards reminds us of the seriousness of taking a stand:

> But he that is become pure in heart, he hates sin; he has an antipathy against it. If he sees any of it hanging about him he abhors himself for it. He seems filthy to himself; he is a burden

unto himself. He abhors the very sight of it and shuns the very appearance of it.[11]

John puts it this way, "And everyone who thus hopes in him purifies himself as he is pure" (1 John 3:3). Being strong in this battle leads to consistency in life and peace of mind.

4. Meditate on "whatever is pure."

It is not just enough to do a "search-and-destroy" mission against impurity in your heart and mind; you must also positively ponder whatever is pure. It is not just enough to rip out the weeds of your mindscape—because you can be sure that if you don't replace them with something better, they will grow back with a vengeance. "Though purity in strictness be only a freedom from filth, yet there are positive qualities and beauties of mind that seem to be implied in pureness of heart; they may be reckoned as part of the pureness of heart because of their contrariety to filthiness."[12]

There is only one truly pure being in the universe: the living and true God. Therefore, you can do no better than to meditate on the perfection of God's character and works. "He delights in the pure and holy exercises of love to God, in the fear of God, in praising and glorifying God, and in pure and holy love to men. He delights in holy thoughts and meditations. Those exercises of the understanding that are holy, in contemplating divine things, are most agreeable to him."[13]

Motivations to these pursuits are found in God's Word. "How can a young man keep his way pure? By guarding it according to your word" (Psalm 119:9). The Scriptures reveal this not in abstraction or otherworldliness but in the incarnate life of God in the Lord Jesus Christ, whose purity of mind and motive was uncontested, not only in his love for his Father but also in his relationships with others. Robert Munger once wrote, "I have discovered through the years that when my attention is centered upon Christ Himself, His purity and power cause impure imaginings to retreat. So he has helped me bring my thoughts into captivity."[14]

In union with him by faith, his Spirit is at work within us to cleanse the filth from the lenses of our minds, that we might truly see the Lord in the perfection of holiness.

"Blessed are the pure in heart, for they shall see God" (Matthew 5:8). Those of faith are destined to a clear vision of him one day. For Paul, wholeness and purity in all of life begins in the thought life: *think about whatever is pure.*"[15]

FOOD FOR THOUGHT

1. Why is thinking about "whatever is pure" important to your mindscape?

2. Why is it difficult to have a pure mind? What forces in today's culture most wear down your purity of mind? Why those in particular?

3. What duplicity and hypocrisy are you most likely to allow to become rooted in your thinking?

4. What steps do you take—or can you take—to prevent you and your family from being exposed to things in the media that might negatively impact your purity of mind?

5. Have you asked God to forgive you and fill you with his Spirit so you can walk in purity of mind? (If not, why not do it now?)

MEMORY VERSE

Matthew 5:8: "Blessed are the pure in heart, for they shall see God."

7

Whatever Is Lovely

❧

"My supremely good Father, beauty of all things beautiful."

Augustine of Hippo[1]

Several years ago my family took a trip to the western United States. There were lots of sights we wanted to see but near the top of the list was the Grand Canyon. I will never forget my sense of awe as I got my first glimpse. It was not merely the vastness of it—with miles between its rims and canyon as far as the eye could see—but its jaw-dropping beauty. The colors of the rock strata seemed to change as the sun moved through the sky, and the Colorado River deep in the gorge below looked like a narrow ribbon winding its way through the valley. All of this was set against the background of the deep blue sky, decorated with billowing white clouds. The loveliness of the world fills me with peace when I think about it. How about you—when you see something beautiful does that also bring to you a sense of peace and joy? That's the way God made us!

Filling our minds with what is lovely is one more way to transform our mindscape and counter the worry weeds that arise through all of life. As we have already seen, Paul has written, "Whatever is true, whatever is noble, whatever is right, whatever is pure." He now teaches us that we should think about "whatever is lovely." What's the most beautiful thing *you've* ever seen? Perhaps it was a magnificent mountain peak capped with snow. Maybe it was an eagle in flight. It may have been your first look at your precious newborn child.

The word Paul uses here is used nowhere else in the Greek New Testament. It is used in Greek literature and is closely related to the word "admirable" that follows in Paul's list. It is a compound word made up of the word for "love" with a prefix meaning "toward." Therefore, "that which attracts love" is pleasing or lovely. The Greek philosophers could not separate the beautiful from the good, the true, and the real, which they saw as all unified in the One. While Plato spoke of this he couldn't put a name on the One—but the Bible does! The One who is the author of all of these, and in whom they find their perfection, is the true and living God. As Al Mohler has written:

> That is not to suggest that nothing else reflects beauty or truth or goodness. It is simply to say that He alone, by virtue of the fact that He is

infinite in all His perfections, is the source and the judge and the end of all that is good, beautiful, true, and real. For as Paul said, from Him and through Him and to Him are all things, to whom be glory forever, Amen.[2]

While we think of creation as beautiful, we must remember that it is beautiful only because its Creator is beautiful. Jonathan Edwards was a student of the beauty of the Lord, and wrote:

The beauty of trees, plants and flowers, with which God has bespangled the face of the earth, is delightful; the beautiful frame of the body of man, especially in its perfection, is astonishing; the beauty of the moon and stars is wonderful; the beauty of the highest heavens is transcendent; the excellency of angels and the saints in light is very glorious; but it is all deformity and darkness in comparison of the brighter glories and beauties of the Creator of all.[3]

God's beauty consists of the perfection of his attributes including his righteousness, holiness, omnipotence, wisdom, mercy, and grace. He is indeed the Creator of the beauty of the universe. Psalm 19 tells us that the beauty of creation speaks of his glory: "The heavens declare the glory of God; and the sky above proclaims his handiwork" (Psalm 19:1). Of course, the consummation of his creative work was the creation of man. After each of the first five days of creation, God proclaimed, "it was good." But after he created the man and the woman on the sixth day he proclaimed, "it was very good" (Genesis 1:31).

As the Creator of the lovely, those things closely related to God were also to be beautiful. When garments were prepared for the high priest, Moses was instructed to "make holy garments for Aaron your brother, for glory and for beauty" (Exodus 28:2). The dwellings representing God's presence among his people were also to be beautiful. When the great temple was built, we are told that Solomon "adorned the house with settings of precious stones" (2 Chronicles 3:6). Francis Schaeffer commented, "There was no pragmatic reason for the precious stones. They had no utilitarian purpose. God simply wanted beauty in the temple. God is interested in beauty."[4] The One who is the perfection and source of beauty must be surrounded by that which is lovely as well.

THE GRAND ENTRANCE OF UGLY

If the Lord is beautiful, and his creation lovely, then where did ugly come from? It was the entrance of sin into the world that marred the beauty of God's creation. The book of Romans teaches that creation is now "subjected to futility," in "bondage to corruption," and full of "groaning" (see Romans 8:20–22). But even so, his glory is still evident. "For his invisible attributes, namely, his eternal power and divine nature, have been clearly perceived, ever since the creation of the world, in the things that have been made. So they are without excuse" (Romans 1:20). The Scriptures also teach that the climactic expression of creation—man made in his image—was marred by sin:

> Adam was made as the image and likeness of God and was given dominion over the earth. He was called to live by faith and obey God's commands. He was created to be the divinely appointed gardener who would turn the whole earth into a garden, and thus, as it were, extend the glory of God. But Adam failed. Instead of exercising the privilege of reflecting God as his image and experiencing in his miniature what it meant for God to be Lord of all—Adam forfeited it.[5]

The scarring of the beauty of mankind is evident not only in human character but also in humanity's efforts to exercise creativity.

THE LOVELY VERSUS THE UGLY

As creatures made in the image of God, though the image is marred, we are still attracted to what is beautiful. There is an inherent consensus among people as to what is beautiful. As creatures made in the image of God, we also are creators. Every culture has its own creative expressions of beauty. Much of this can be seen in what we call the "arts," particularly in art and music. Unfortunately, sin has impacted these areas of life as well.

Plato was right when he saw the need for the connection between the beautiful, the good, the true, and the real. We have been given a glimpse into what can happen when there is a disconnect between the beautiful, the good, the true, and the real. Hans Rookmaaker and Francis Schaeffer have written extensively on what has happened to the arts, as they have become expressions of increasingly secular and irrational perspective pervasive in Western culture. For example, Jackson Pollock reflected meaninglessness and despair in going about his "art" by placing canvases on the floor and dripping paint on them from cans swinging above them. This was intended to communicate that "chance" rules. But even then he couldn't escape the order of God's universe—because the laws of gravity and motion dictated the movement of the paint!

Some modern music isn't much better. Dispensing with ordinary standards of meter, melody, and harmony, modern composers have made their statements as well. Arnold Schoenberg came along and gave us twelve-tone music with no resolution as a picture of his despairing worldview. Following him was his student John Cage. Cage believed that everything has come about by chance and he expressed this in his "music." He is probably best known for his composition 4'33", which was debuted by David Tudor in a recital of contemporary piano music in 1952. He came onto the stage, sat at the piano, and lifted the piano's lid. He played no notes but sat in silence. Then he closed the lid. He repeated this twice more without playing any notes, after which he stood up and left the stage. You see, the title 4'33" signified four minutes and thirty-three seconds of silence. The artist did hold a stopwatch as he turned the pages of the score! Isn't it interesting that Cage's work still depended on the orderliness of time?

Though Cage died in 1992, his "music" lives on. His composition *Organ2/ASLSP* is being performed right now in Halberstadt, Germany, and will not finish until 2640—a total elapsed time of 639 years![6] It began on September 5, 2001, but the first year and one half was total silence. The first chord was not sounded until February 5, 2003. It did not progress to the second chord until January 5, 2005. Small bags of sand hold down the keys for their lengthy performance. The first "movement" will last seventy-one years. If you didn't figure it out, "ASLSP" stands for "As SLow aS Possible!"

All of this begs the question, "Is this really music?" or "Is this really art?" Schaeffer notes, "The more it tends to be only an intellectual statement, rather than a work of art, the more it becomes anti-art."[7] The bigger problem is that the statement is also often anti-God, anti-order, and anti-beauty. "Beauty used to be one of the artist's highest priorities; now for many artists it is among the lowest priorities, if it is even a criterion for artwork at all."[8]

Of course, the ultimate evidence of the impact of sin on God's creation is the entrance of death itself. Because man sins, he dies. The very climax of the created order is destined for destruction unless there is intervention. Artistic expressions can then be the cry of a heart in despair of death or a rebellious fist in the face of God. The good news is that the Lord has not left us in this condition.

THE ULTIMATE BEAUTIFICATION PROJECT

The author of beauty has embarked on a mission not only to redeem humanity but all creation with it. If sin is the ultimate destroyer of whatever is lovely, Jesus came to restore it. Being unstained by sin he was the perfection of divinity and humanity, as John wrote, "In the beginning was the Word, and the Word was with God, and the Word was God.... And the Word became flesh and dwelt among us, and we have seen his glory, glory as of the only Son from the Father, full of grace and truth" (John 1:1, 14). Jesus's purpose in coming into the world was to glorify his Father through perfect obedience and to destroy the ugliness of sin and death.

In one of the most remarkable mysteries of all, the perfect and beautiful Savior took upon himself the ugliness of sin on the cross for all who will believe in him. Remarkably, he laid down his life voluntarily. Death had no claim on him, but he submitted to its penalty for our sakes. He rose from the dead and ascended into heaven conquering sin, death, and the grave. Those who believe are completely forgiven. "There is therefore now no condemnation for those who are in Christ Jesus" (Romans 8:1). The restoration project has begun.

This restoration is an ongoing work in two parts. It includes the demolition of our old sinful habits, and then the replacement of them with new ones as we are progressively conformed to the image of Jesus. This can seem like a painstakingly slow process but don't be discouraged—the result is worth it!

Some of the most beautiful frescoes in the world are found in the Vatican's Sistine Chapel. Michelangelo took six years to complete them in the early sixteenth century. Over the years, however, layers of grime began to obscure their beauty; their very survival became at risk. In 1979 it was determined that these magnificent works of art would be cleaned and restored. The first step was to apply a cleaning solvent to a postage-stamp size section of one of the frescoes; the experiment succeeded. It took twenty years to complete the project—more than twice as long to restore them as it did to paint them in the first place! The results have been amazing. At the time of its completion, the Governor of Vatican City said, "This renovation and the expertise of the restorers allows us to contemplate the paintings as if we had been given the chance of being present when they were first shown."[9]

The renovation the Lord has begun in your own heart and mind will continue throughout your life. Amazingly, when he is finished, you will be even *better* than new because you will be remade in the likeness of Jesus. In the meantime his Spirit has been given to help us remove the grime of sin and restore the image of God in the likeness of Jesus. The process will be complete only when you meet Jesus in glory or when he comes back to make everything new and beautiful again.

The same text that speaks of the impact of sin on creation speaks of its restoration: "For the creation waits with eager longing for the revealing of the sons of God. For the creation was subjected to futility, not willingly, but because of him who subjected it, in hope that the creation itself will be set free from its bondage to corruption and obtain the freedom of the glory of the children of God" (Romans 8:19–21). I also appreciate the words of Owen Strachan and Doug Sweeney on this subject:

The Lord in fact had crafted a great plan by which to express His beauty and make His glory known. He existed as the resplendent one, but did not content Himself with mere self-appreciation of His beauty. Instead, He set in motion an arc of glory that began with Himself, moved to the creation, continued with the incarnation of Christ, moved next to the church, the bride of Christ, and is consummated in heaven, where the Holy Trinity dwells.[10]

BEAUTIFYING YOUR MINDSCAPE

You may be thinking: All of this talk about beauty and restoration is wonderful, but how does all of it apply when I'm in the middle of a rough day?

Here's a good place to start: Whenever you're overcome with worries, with concern about all the things that could go wrong, ask for the Spirit to fill your mind with what is lovely instead. Then, by faith, turn your mind to the loveliness of Christ. That might seem a bit abstract, so consider how King David lived this out in his life.

King David had a lot of problems. It seemed as if there was always someone who was out to get him. It wasn't just the Philistines, either. Sometimes those who sought his life were those who should have been grateful (Saul) or those in his own family (Absalom). In many of the psalms we have a window into what David thought about when he was in trouble, and we can learn much from them as we face our own troubles.

Psalm 27 has always been an encouragement to me when I face a worrisome situation. As David reflects on being surrounded by enemies and evildoers this prayer rises to the Lord: "One thing have I asked of the LORD, that will I seek after: that I may dwell in the house of the LORD all the days of my life, to gaze upon the beauty of the LORD and to inquire in his temple" (Psalm 27:4). The word translated "beauty" (*goam*) speaks of something that is pleasant and delightful. For David, this beauty consisted of everything wonderful that he had come to know about the Lord—his holiness, righteousness, faithfulness, grace, and love. As humans, we are *attracted* to whatever we delight in and whatever we find pleasant, especially in times when we need comfort. David's delight is in the Lord, and so it is the beauty of the Lord in which he finds comfort.

A few verses later this becomes even more personal: "You have said, 'Seek my face.' My heart says to you, 'Your face, LORD, do I seek'" (Psalm 27:8). David was interested in the dwelling of God because this was where he could find the Lord himself, the one in whom he delighted. What was the result? David was confident that the Lord would take care of him and that he would be given the strength he needed as he awaited the Lord's intervention. "Wait for the LORD; be strong, and let your heart take courage; wait for the LORD!" (Psalm 27:14).

If it's true that we're *attracted* to whatever we delight in and whatever we find pleasant—especially in times when we need comfort, in what do you take your delight (and comfort)? Is your delight in the beauty of the Lord, or is it in something else? How do you know? The answer is found in what you run to for comfort or for stress relief. People talk about "comfort food"—or more to the point, describe themselves as "stress eaters." For others, stress relief is found at the expense of others in angry rants or moodiness. For some there is an even darker manifestation as they turn to other forms of self-satisfaction with hopes of escaping the pain. Sexual fantasies, drug or alcohol-induced euphoria, and even shopping sprees are all false fixes.

The problem with all of these "comforts" is that the relief is always temporary. The momentary satisfaction passes, and you are right back in the middle of it again—except now it's worse because you have the added guilt of having eaten twenty-five Oreos® or because you need to go back and apologize for being such a jerk to your loved one or coworker.

In thinking about "whatever is lovely" as an antidote to worry, of course, you should fill your mind with things that are aesthetically beautiful—such as beautiful art, music, or the wonders of nature. But even as you do these things, be sure to allow them all to point you to the one who is Creator of the natural world and the giver of human creativity that produces works pleasing to the eye, ear, and heart. So yes, when you're stressed listen to music, go to a museum, or take a walk in the woods—but use all these things to point you to the One who is truly beautiful. Seek his presence as you go, and meditate on his majesty, holiness, and faithfulness.

FROM MINDSCAPE TO LIFESCAPE

As a child of God made in his image you should make good use of the creative gifts he has given you. If you're a musician, use your talent to compose or perform to his glory. As I already mentioned, I play the tuba. What motivates me the most as I anticipate a performance with The Westminster Brass or other groups has been to consider the "audience of One," remembering that my ultimate goal and concern should be to please the Lord. After all, he is the one who gave the gift in the first place!

Of course, my hope is that the performance will lift up listeners' hearts and spirits to the Lord as well. David Kim, concertmaster of the acclaimed Philadelphia Orchestra, has expressed this principle quite well: "Despite success and prominence as a musician, I was long blind to my one true Audience. I suppose I could even say that all playing was in vain. But with truth came purpose, and today I play to honor Him who blessed me with His gifts."[11]

If you're an artist, use your talent to express your praise and worship to him. Be committed to honor him with excellence and beauty in what you do. Schaeffer writes, "Christian art is the expression of the whole life of the whole person who is a Christian. What a Christian portrays in his art is the totality of life."[12] When you do this it is part of your testimony to the world, which brings glory to your Lord. As Phil Ryken has said:

> Christian art is redemptive and this is its highest purpose. Art is always an interpretation of reality in its total aspect, including the hope that has come into the world through the life, death, and resurrection of Jesus Christ. Rather

than giving in to meaningless and despair, Christian artists know that there is a way out. Thus they create images of grace, awakening a desire for the new heavens and the new earth by anticipating the possibilities of redemption in Christ.[13]

An important element of the consideration of "whatever is lovely" is your consideration of how you can use your life, your gifts, and your talents to beautify the world around you. Schaeffer wrote, "No work of art is more important than the Christian's own life, and every Christian is called upon to be an artist in this sense. He may have no gift in writing, no gift of composing or singing, but each one has the gift of creativity in terms of the way he lives his life. The Christian's life is to be a thing of truth and also a thing of beauty in the midst of a lost and dying world."[14]

In the film *A Beautiful Mind*, Russell Crowe depicted the mathematician John Nash, who was eventually awarded the Nobel Prize for Economics for his equilibrium theory. The irony of the film's title is that though Nash was a remarkably gifted intellectual, it was the descent of his mind into paranoia that led to the cessation of his career. In our world, people tend to consider the beautiful mind to be the one of genius and high intelligence quotient. However, the truly beautiful mind is the one that reflects on whatever is lovely, especially on the beauty of the Lord, his works in the world, and how their lives and work can reflect that loveliness in a world of ugliness.

FOOD FOR THOUGHT

1. In your own words, why is it important to reflect upon "whatever is lovely"?

2. How have you observed sin impacting the "lovely"? Provide some recent examples from art, music, or elsewhere.

3. Read Psalm 27 and identify how David is helped as he meditates on the beauty of the Lord. How does this reflection help *you* to meditate on the beauty of the Lord as well?

4. If beauty is what we delight in, and what we delight in is where we flee for comfort, where do you look for comfort? Do those things truly comfort? If not, what other issues result from indulging in those "delights"?

5. In what ways have you seen the Lord's beautification and restoration project underway in your life? How has that helped in other areas of your life that are still in need of restoration?

6. How might you use your artistic gifts to glorify the Lord? Or, if you're not artistic, how might you, in Francis Schaeffer's words, "[have] the gift of creativity in terms of the way" you live your life?

MEMORY VERSE

Psalm 27:4: "One thing have I asked of the LORD, that will I seek after: that I may dwell in the house of the LORD all the days of my life, to gaze upon the beauty of the LORD and to inquire in his temple."

8

Whatever Is Admirable

～

"To have our minds so filled with spiritual desires and thoughts as was the mind of Christ, is the most important duty in the Christian life."

John Owen[1]

Everybody admires somebody. For me, Dad was always at the top of the list. So many prominent people of the day reminded me of him. When it came to golf, it was Arnold Palmer. Bob Hope's humor always reminded me of Dad. Others who made me think of him were Jimmy Stewart and humorist-statesman Will Rogers. Dad's work ethic was epic, though he never compromised family or church commitments for his job. His absolute devotion to my mother is also something I've always admired.

The power of admiration is that it fuels our aspirations of who we want to be and what we want to do. Admiring others turns our minds from ourselves (always a good thing and often a source of our worries!) and gives us goals. Reflecting on what was admirable about Dad has always served me well.

The word translated "admirable" (*euphemos;* Philippians 4:8 NIV) is found only in this one place in the Greek New Testament. It is a compound word with the root word meaning "sound" and a prefix meaning "good"—literally, "good sounding." There is a musical instrument that takes its name directly from this word, the euphonium—which, when played correctly (and, as noted earlier, when it doesn't have a rotting piece of corn inside it), makes a beautiful sound.

How are we to understand this as we consider "whatever is admirable" in a mindscape designed to counter worry? Perhaps a few comments from others will help. Gordon Fee writes that "it represents the kind of conduct that is worth considering because it is well-spoken of by people in general."[2] I-Jin Loh and Eugene Nida describe it as "what people can always think good about."[3]

We have been created to be admirers. We must be sure to admire what is truly admirable. But where can truly admirable things be found? The question can be answered in terms of the vistas we've already examined: whatever is true, noble, right, pure, and lovely. These are all worthy of admiration when properly understood. The use of the word indicates things that can be generally admired by all people. Let's expand our mindscapes further and think of some more things that fit the category of "whatever is admirable."

ADMIRABLE CHARACTER

You may have seen the story of Mitchell Marcus, a special-needs student at Coronado High School in El Paso, Texas. He loved basketball but couldn't play well enough to be on the team, so he became the team manager. Week after week for three years he faithfully fulfilled his duties, never imagining what his head coach, Peter Morales, had in mind.

Coach Morales was determined to put Mitchell in a game, regardless of the score. Before the last game of the season Morales told Mitchell to suit up, and with ninety seconds left he sent Mitchell into the game. Not only did Mitchell get to play, but his teammates were determined that he score a basket. With the crowd shouting "Mitchell! Mitchell! Mitchell!" his teammates passed the ball to him on every possession, but he couldn't make the shot. It appeared that only part of his dream was going to be realized. Then, something quite amazing occurred. There were only thirteen seconds left when Jonathan Montanez, *a member of the opposing team,* inbounded the ball, shouted "Mitchell!" and passed the ball to him. Mitchell turned around, and with time expiring took the shot. Off the glass and into the net it went!

Mitchell scored and the crowd stormed onto the floor, hoisted him onto their shoulders shouting "Mitchell! Mitchell! Mitchell!" When asked why he passed the ball to Mitchell, Montanez said, "Growing up, my parents taught me to treat others the way I would want to be treated. I just thought Mitchell deserved his chance."[4]

As you read this story, did a tear come to your eyes? There are so many admirable elements in this story: the coach's determination to play Mitchell; the attempts of his teammates to help Mitchell score; Mitchell's commitment to serve the team for three years even though he couldn't play; and the heart of an opposing player who did not want to see Mitchell miss his chance.

Stories like this are kept for the last five minutes of the evening news. (By the way, after seeing this story on the news, the chancellor of Texas Tech University called Jonathan Montanez and offered him a scholarship to study there!) You will notice that at the root of *every* such story are Judeo-Christian values such as selflessness, love, and service. People don't usually admire others who are selfish, hateful, or self-serving. These types usually get on the evening news for other reasons. On the other hand, stories like Mitchell's are inspiring and admirable. Since we aspire to what we admire, it encourages us to be selfless in our service to others.

ADMIRABLE PERFORMANCES

There are times when ordinary people accomplish extraordinary things when put in difficult circumstances. Everybody remembers Captain Chesley "Sully" Sullenberger's skill in saving 155 lives aboard US Airways flight 1549 as he had to ditch the jet in the icy waters of the Hudson River after the engines were disabled by a bird strike. But you might not have heard of Captain Tadeusz Wrona who faced a similar dilemma. In late 2011 he was piloting a LOT Polish Airlines Boeing 767 with 230 passengers on a flight from Newark to Warsaw.

On approach, the electrical system for the landing gear failed and they were unable to get "wheels down." They circled the airport for more than an hour, but the wheels would not come down. Captain Wrona dumped the remaining fuel and told the passengers to brace themselves for a crash landing. He was going to attempt to land the giant plane on its belly on the runway. With most fearing the worst, he brought the jet in perfectly as it skidded to a halt. Everyone was safe and thrilled to be alive! When acclaimed as a hero he said, "I am absolutely sure that each of us would have done it the same way, and that the result would have been the same."[5]

It also seems as though genuine heroes generally reject the acclaim, as did Captain Wrona. We see not only competence, but also humility to go along with it. When someone performs their work with such excellence, it is truly admirable. No one that I know admires incompetence. No one that I know admires someone who brags about all of his or her accomplishments. In fact, I try to get away from such folks as quickly as possible!

Paul writes, "Whatever you do, work heartily, as for the Lord and not for men, knowing that from the Lord you will receive the inheritance as your reward. You are serving the Lord Christ" (Colossians 3:23–24). Is this your attitude toward your work? Whether you are a student, a housewife, or a white- or blue-collar worker, are you doing your work as unto the Lord? You might not think that anyone notices, but the Lord does. Soon others will, too. When you are "noticed" what is your attitude? "The fear of the LORD is instruction in wisdom, and humility comes before honor" (Proverbs 15:33).

ADMIRABLE RELATIONSHIPS

In a world characterized by loneliness, alienation, and isolation, admirable relationships have become increasingly rare. Sure, we have social media, but have you noticed that Facebook posts, tweets, and blogs just seem to provide more opportunities to display how dysfunctional we really are?

Networking might be increasing the *number* of those with whom we're connected, but those connections are more superficial. Stephen Marche addressed this development in an article in *The Atlantic* entitled "Is Facebook Making Us Lonely?":

> Yet within this world of instant and absolute communication, unbounded by limits of time or space, we suffer from unprecedented alienation. We have never been more detached from one another, or lonelier. In a world consumed by ever more novel modes of socializing, we have less and less actual society. We live in an accelerating contradiction: the more connected we become, the lonelier we are. We were promised a global village; instead we inhabit the drab cul-de-sacs and endless freeways of a vast suburb of information.[6]

Marche also cites Sherry Turkle, a professor of computer culture at MIT, who wrote the book *Alone Together* in 2011: "These days, insecure in our relationships and anxious about intimacy, we look to technology for ways to be in relationships and protect ourselves from them at the same time. The ties we form through the Internet are not, in the end, the ties that bind. But they are the ties that preoccupy. We don't want to intrude on each other, so instead we constantly intrude on each other, but not in 'real time.'"[7]

Researchers are also concerned that social media has led to a rise in narcissism. After all, doesn't every social medium operate under the presumption that everyone else must be interested in what *I* have to say and what *I'm* doing? Certainly everyone will be interested in the pictures showing what *I* had for breakfast or what *I* am reading right now. "Narcissism is the flip side of loneliness, and either condition is a fighting retreat from the messy reality of other people."[8] And yet, the messy reality of other people is exactly what we need.

The bottom line is that in terms of relating to other people, you just can't beat the real thing: actually *meeting with* them and *talking to* them face-to-face. This is the only way that we can have healthy relationships. A new status symbol these days is the number of Twitter *followers* people have. I would suggest that a far better mark of relational health is how many deep *friendships* they have. Deeply committed friendships are so rare these days that they are truly admirable.

Among the most important relationships are those in the family. How many families do you know that are admirable? How many marriages could you identify as ones which you emulate? As I have argued in a previous book,[9] in order to have a healthy marriage you must spend time with your spouse, so you can truly get to know one another. This enables you to relate to one another at a heart level needed for marital oneness. In order to raise children to be mature adults, parents must spend time with them, talking with them and truly getting to know them. It is in talking with you that your children develop an ability to respect and relate to other adults.

We are blessed in our church to have several couples who have been married for more than fifty years and at least one couple married more than sixty years. I have truly admired these amazing people who have kept their vows to God and to one another for a lifetime. It is a great example for other couples in our church to see what marital faithfulness looks like. It's also great for the children and young people to see that God's plan for marriage is not merely possible but preferable.

A few years ago I sat with one of these dear couples as the husband was dying after a long battle with cancer. He took his wife's hand into his, looked into her eyes and said, "It's been delicious." I admired the remarkable love in those words, and I always will.

EXPRESS YOUR ADMIRATION

When you come across those people whose character, performance, or relationship you admire—tell them!

I recently met another man for whom I developed an instant admiration. It was a busy day at the seminary and I saw an older man walking around campus with several folks in tow. I happened to be in the administration building when they entered. As he peeked into the admissions office I overheard him say, "This is where we used to have chapel." I asked him if he was an alumnus and he said that he was, after which he introduced his family members who were all beaming with pride. He recounted that he had graduated many decades earlier and was now retired; this was his first return trip to campus since graduation. He enumerated several churches where he had served through the years and had determined to show his family "where it all began."

I can't begin to tell you how much I admired that man, *and I told him so.* In these days when so many are leaving ministry due to moral failure, toxic relationships, or just plain old burnout, this man was a trophy of God's grace. I wished him and his family well and told him that if he was ever going to be on campus again that I would love to have him come and speak to one of my classes. I meant it! Our students need to see examples of men who have finished strong in the ministry.

Another simple example of this is the pizza shop we frequent. We first became familiar with Go-Go Pizza when we first moved to town nearly thirty years ago. They sold their pizza from a window just outside the doors of the 69th Street Terminal and it was amazing. The pizzas were so big that they barely fit in a very large box—and more importantly, they tasted great! When the terminal was being renovated they moved across the street, and we followed; when they moved back to the terminal, we followed them back. The pizza is so good that our out-of-town children request that we order some as soon as they return to town. I make a point of telling the workers how much we enjoy their pizza—and not to get a price break! It's enabled us to develop friendships over the years, which led to one of the workers coming to Christ and joining our church. When you see someone who is admirable in their work or their character or their relationships, *tell them*.

FROM MINDSCAPE TO LIFESCAPE

What you admire is very important because *you aspire to what you admire*. In the examples described throughout this chapter, didn't your admiration fuel an aspiration? Didn't you want to be as thoughtful as the student who inbounded the ball to Mitchell Marcus, to do your job as well and as humbly as Polish pilot Wrona, to finish your work with integrity as did the retired pastor, or to improve your relationship with your spouse and your children?

The old saying is that "imitation is the highest form of flattery." When I was in college, the leader of our campus ministry was a very charismatic leader. We emulated and imitated him. In fact, one of my friends began to take on some of the nuances of the leader's Midwestern accent—hints of which you can still hear today in his conversation.

To ponder whatever is admirable in your mindscape is important because it takes your mind off of what might be wrong and focuses on what can actually become your new reality as you walk in faith, grounded in whatever is true according to the Scriptures in these various categories. And, as mentioned earlier, all of these admirable examples reflect biblical principles in some way.

Our ultimate goal is not to be admired by others but to see others admire the One who is the source of any admirable qualities we have. Jesus put it this way, "Let your light shine before others, so that they may see your good works and give glory to your Father who is in heaven" (Matthew 5:16). As we grow in our admiration (or worship) of the Lord, we aspire to be like him; he makes us like him through the Spirit; and this brings him glory.

Unfortunately, the things that we admire tend to be much more superficial and self-satisfying. Here are a few traps to avoid as we look at the dark side of "whatever is admirable."

THE DARK SIDE OF ADMIRATION

As with each of the vistas of the new mindscape, there are weeds that can sometimes look very much like the real thing. I'm sure someone you know (or perhaps even you!) picked some poison ivy, thinking that it was "pretty" or that it was something else. Unfortunately, the itchy blisters that followed proved its power to irritate. In our sinfulness, admiration can deteriorate into some very dangerous weeds. Here are just a few of those weeds, and ways we can attack them:

The Weed of Covetousness.

Covetousness is *admiring something that belongs to someone else and wishing it were yours.* We are naturally "admirers." Unfortunately, in our sinful state it is not enough to admire something that belongs to someone else; we often cross the line and actually wish that it *was* ours. Do you see how quickly then our wanting what we don't have crowds out the peace of Christ and leads to worry and anxiety? The discontented heart is a heart that is worried about many things (Luke 10:41).

This weed makes God's top ten list. "You shall not covet your neighbor's house; you shall not covet your neighbor's wife, or his male servant, or his female servant, or his ox, or his donkey, or anything that is your neighbor's" (Exodus 20:17). This just about covers everything. We shouldn't long for our neighbor's lifestyle (his house). We shouldn't lust after our neighbor's wife. We shouldn't long for our neighbor's productivity (ox or donkey). Just so nothing is forgotten, the Lord adds, "or anything that is your neighbor's." The Westminster Larger Catechism gives this summary of what is forbidden in the tenth commandment: "The sins forbidden in the tenth commandment are, discontentment with our own estate; envying and grieving at the good of our neighbor, together with all inordinate motions and affections to anything that is his."[10]

This gives us a clue as to how to replace the weed of covetousness. There is a federal urban redevelopment plan called "Weed and Seed." Our church in Upper Darby, Pennsylvania, is in a "Weed and Seed" neighborhood. The concept is to get rid of the weeds and to replace them with good seeds that will enhance the health of the neighborhood. An example of weeds would be crime and blight. We are hoping that our neighbors consider our church to be a good seed!

Covetousness looks at what someone else has and concludes, "I don't have enough." The seed to replace the weed of covetousness, then, is *contentment*.

The Seed of Contentment

Contentment is being completely satisfied with what the Lord has provided, whether it is my lifestyle, my spouse, my possessions, or anything else. This doesn't mean that we don't work hard to improve our lot in life or to grow our business, but it does mean being at peace *with what I have now.* The Westminster Larger Catechism, again, provides some helpful words: "The duties required in the tenth commandment are, such a full contentment with our own condition, and such a charitable frame of the whole soul toward our neighbor, as that all our inward motions and affections touching him, tend unto, and further all that good which is his."[11]

While sitting in a Roman jail, in this very letter to the Philippians, Paul could write, "I have learned the secret of being content in any and every situation, whether well fed or hungry, whether living in plenty or in want" (Philippians 4:12 NIV). Failure to be content in the Lord can lead to covetousness and to the very poisonous weed of envy and all of the anxiety that goes along with wanting what we don't have.

The Weed of Envy:

Envy is *admiring what belongs to someone else and then resenting them for having it.*

In both of the above Larger Catechism answers there are some hints at the progression from covetousness to envy. In what the tenth commandment *forbids*, the writers include, "envying and grieving at the good of our neighbor, together with all inordinate motions and affections to anything that is his." In what the tenth commandment *requires,* the writers include, "such a charitable frame of the whole soul toward our neighbor, as that all our inward motions and affections touching him, tend unto, and further all that good which is his." It is very difficult to want what someone else has without impacting how you feel about its owners. Envy is when covetousness gets personal. Here is the equation:

Covetousness + Resentment = Envy

It is a wonderful thing to admire someone else, but very dangerous when you begrudge them for what they have. The categories of envy, therefore, are the same as they are for the categories of covetousness. I suppose it's possible to covet what someone has without envying him or her, but it's not very likely. It is certainly *not possible* to envy someone without the groundwork of covetousness being laid in advance. All of this is the dark side of admiration and a recipe for worry.

Here's how it works. We admire someone's expertise on the job, but it becomes covetousness when you wish that you were as competent. Now, add resentment toward that person and you've got envy. Here's another example. You admire someone's "looks" and you wish you looked like that (covetousness), but it gets personal when you resent them for it (envy). One last example. You admire someone else's ministry but then wish it were yours (covetousness). Next, you can't imagine why God would bless him and not you. You resent *him* and envy sets in.

Of course, the danger in all of this is that resentment rarely remains merely in our minds. It "acts out" in the way we treat those we envy and the way we talk about them to others. Some take it further and find ways to undermine the person they envy. This can really get nasty, as James portrays it, "You desire and do not have, so you murder. You covet and cannot obtain, so you fight and quarrel" (James 4:2). We've all seen how this looks in our children. Imagine one child receives a special toy. At first, big brother Billy feigns happiness for his little brother, but soon Billy says, "I want one, too" (covetousness). It doesn't take long before Billy's resentment turns personal (envy) and he tries to forcibly secure the item from his little brother. It's not a pretty scene.

One of the clearest examples of this in Scripture is Joseph and his brothers. There's no doubt that Jacob showed favoritism to Joseph. He was the son of Rachel, whom Jacob truly loved. This didn't matter to his brothers; they coveted that attention and love and it didn't take long until it turned personal (envy) and then to hatred. "But when his brothers saw that their father loved him more than all his brothers, they hated him and could not speak peacefully to him" (Genesis 37:4). Of course, this wasn't Joseph's fault, but it didn't matter. Though they contemplated killing him, they settled for selling him as a slave to Ishmaelite traders. As far as they were concerned, he was as good as dead. In the meantime the brothers' actions led to years of dealing with their distraught, grieving father, which only magnified the underlying guilt for what they had done. They also lived with the worry that they would be "found out." Of course, the Lord had other plans for Joseph and his brothers! (Read Genesis 37–50 for the entirety of this remarkable story.)

We can all think of times when our own envy was acted out against those for whom our admiration deteriorated into covetousness and envy. If contentment is the seed to replace the weed of covetousness, what then is the seed to replace the weed of envy?

The Seed of Love

If you love someone, you rejoice when they are blessed. Once again, our selections from the Larger Catechism help us understand how to keep admiration from disintegrating into covetousness and envy. Instead of "grieving at the good of our neighbor" we should have "such a charitable frame of the whole soul toward our neighbor, as that all our inward motions and affections touching him, tend unto, and further all that good which is his." We should love our neighbor so much that we rejoice when things go well with him. We need to embrace the fact that God has given that person her good looks or his giftedness to be proficient at his work. As for ministry envy, the Lord gifted that person and has chosen to bless his ministry at this time. You should rejoice that the Lord is doing so. When we do so, this is *godly* admiration, and it is a good example of practicing the second great commandment: Love your neighbor as yourself. Unfortunately, we are so committed to ourselves and to our own comfort and advancement that we are only interested in loving and admiring ourselves.

Ultimately, the weeds of covetousness and envy betray the existence of a much more deeply rooted weed—resentment against God. When our admiration turns to covetousness we are inwardly expressing that

God hasn't given us what we deserve. The decline of covetousness to envy challenges the sovereignty of God in how he manages the universe. We're really saying, "If I were God, I would not have given *this* blessing to *that* person." Do you see how pitiful we are?

Our only hope is to rejoice in the Lord and to rest in his wisdom as he unfolds his plan for us and for others. Do you remember the end of the Joseph story? The Lord exalted Joseph to a position of greatness in Egypt and gave him wisdom to prepare for a devastating famine. Not only were the Egyptian people saved but so were many others, including Joseph's brothers.

When his brothers *were* found out through these amazing divine developments in Joseph's rise to power, they were afraid that he was going to take revenge. Do you see how closely fear is allied with envy? But how amazing was the grace that Joseph offered his brothers when he said "Do not fear, for am I in the place of God? As for you, you meant evil against me, but God meant it for good, to bring it about that many people should be kept alive, as they are today" (Genesis 50:19–20). After all that he had experienced, Joseph saw that through it all God was at work. Do you believe this as you're tempted to compare what you have with what someone else has? Or do you just stew with envy and worry about it?

I think you'll agree that when we merely admire the things of this world, we're settling for a life less than the one the Lord intended. If what you admire is superficial, *you'll* be superficial. If you only admire cold hard possessions, you'll develop a cold hard heart; those possessions will become a major feature of your mindscape and obscure both the goodness of God and the needs of others.

I like what David Powlison wrote about this, "*Covetous* greed will make you angry and manipulative. . . . *Complacent, satisfied* greed makes you care less about what really matters; because it lulls you to sleep.... *Anxious* greed [will make you worry]" (emphasis original).[12] It doesn't matter where you move it—if what you admire is superficial, it will always trouble you and distract you from focusing on what is truly admirable.

FOOD FOR THOUGHT

1. How do the things you admire affect your mindscape? Be specific.

2. "You aspire to what you admire." Do you agree with this statement? Think of some personal examples that illustrate this.

3. Think of an example in each of the following categories, and relate how each of these examples have inspired you:
  • Admirable character

  • Admirable performances

  • Admirable relationships

4. What are the dangers of admiring unworthy things? What impact might this have on your life? Where have you already seen this impact, and how can you address it now?

5. How do covetousness and envy add stress to your mindscape?

MEMORY VERSE

Matthew 5:16: "In the same way, let your light shine before others, so that they may see your good works and give glory to your Father who is in heaven."

9

If Anything Is Excellent
or Praiseworthy

"The climax of His happiness is the delight He takes in the echoes of His excellence in the praises of the saints."

John Piper[1]

As we conclude this remarkable tour of the truly beautiful mind, Paul doesn't finish with a whimper but with a bang. There are two concepts presented together in this chapter. It is clear from the structure of the phrase that these two together represent the culmination of what's gone before.

You'll notice that each of the earlier vistas was introduced by "whatever" (*"whatever* is true, *whatever* is noble, *whatever* is right,"* etc.). However, for these last two, the language changes to *and* ("if anything is excellent or praiseworthy") and are joined by the conjunction *and* (literally, "if anything is excellent *and* if anything is praiseworthy"). Paul is right in putting the terms together. If something is truly excellent it is worthy of praise. If something is worthy of praise it must be excellent. As William Hendriksen has observed, "Anything at all that is a matter of moral and spiritual excellence, so that it is the proper object of praise, is the right pasture for the Christian to graze in. Nothing that is of a contrary nature is the right food for his thought."[2] Our primary focus, then, will be on excellence.

The first word that Paul uses was one with which his readers would have been quite familiar. The word translated "excellent" (*arête*) is right out of Greek philosophy. But while Paul's readers would have been quite familiar with the term, they may have been surprised to find it in this letter. In fact, it appears nowhere else in his epistles. Why now?

The word translated "excellent" is the Greek word for "virtue." It was "the most comprehensive Greek term for moral excellence and the central theme of Greek ethics."[3] The Greek philosophers themselves couldn't agree on what it meant. Plato argued that virtue was a *single* thing, but others spoke of a *plurality* of virtues. Most, however, believed that the purpose of practicing virtue was to become happy. We have already seen how frustrating and nerve-wracking the practice of virtue can be when it's left up to us. Maybe that's the reason we aren't happy but stressed.

Paul's intention, however, is not to send his readers running back to Plato; "what he intends, of course, is that 'virtue' be filled with Christian content."[4] Once again, we have to see that true "excellence" can only be found in the Lord. The consummate excellence of God is expressed in biblical words such as holiness, righteousness, and glory. We have come full circle. The genuine standard of excellence is "whatever is true, whatever is noble, whatever is right," according to our Creator and as revealed in his Word.

Paul's friend, the apostle Peter, sheds light on what excellence looks like. While Paul uses the word "excellent" only one time, Peter uses it four times. In the remarkable opening words of his second letter, Peter reminds his readers that "His divine power has granted to us all things that pertain to life and godliness, through the knowledge of him who called us to his own glory and *excellence*" (2 Peter 1:3, emphasis added). Other translations render it *"by"* his own glory and excellence (NIV, NASB). This is worth noting. One rendering ("to") sees God's excellence as the goal of our calling, that to which we are called. The other rendering ("by") sees the focus on God's excellence as the *means* by which he calls us to himself. The grammar of the phrase supports either one. Both are true.

As to the first rendering—that is, in light of the goal of our calling—"excellence" is an appropriate word to describe the glory of the Lord. The Scriptures are filled with superlative descriptions of the excellence of our God. He is the wisest, holiest, most righteous, and most merciful of all! As we are called *to* his glory and excellence, we now see God's glory as we had not seen it before. Shouldn't we fill the vistas of our mind-scape with thoughts of God's excellence, as revealed in what he has created and what he has revealed in his Word? Think about how much this would help when we're bogged down in the worries of this world. These thoughts would give us buoyancy that would give us a new perspective on the problems of each day.

As to the second rendering, excellence is a wonderful way to express *the way* God has called us to himself. When it is left to man to ponder a way of access to God, the default approach is working up his own excellence or virtue (remember the Greeks!).

Unfortunately, man's best efforts always come up short. A great example of the bankruptcy of human effort is Benjamin Franklin's effort to improve himself, as he writes in his *Autobiography.* Interestingly enough his "virtue" project was inspired by a sermon on the very text upon which this book is based! Having heard a sermon on Philippians 4:8, Franklin was completely frustrated. The five applications that the preacher brought from the text were: 1. Keeping holy the Sabbath day. 2. Being diligent in reading the Scriptures. 3. Attending public worship. 4. Partaking of the Sacrament. 5. Paying a due respect to God's ministers. Franklin observed that "as they were not the kind of good things that I expected from that text, I despaired of ever meeting with them from any other, was disgusted, and attended his preaching no more."[5] I can't say that I blame him! Though the things the preacher spoke of were certainly good things, they don't seem to be the natural applications flowing from this text.

What did Dr. Franklin do in response? He decided to become the model of virtue all by himself. "It was about this time I conceiv'd the bold and arduous project of arriving at moral perfection. I wish'd to live without committing any fault at any time; I would conquer all that either natural inclination, custom, or company might lead me into. As I knew, or thought I knew, what was right and wrong, I did not see why I might not always do the one and avoid the other."[6] How did he determine to do this? First of all he would have to come up with a list of virtues. After much study he settled on twelve. Here they are, along with his descriptions of each:

1. TEMPERANCE. Eat not to dullness; drink not to elevation.
2. SILENCE. Speak not but what may benefit others or yourself; avoid trifling conversation.
3. ORDER. Let all your things have their places; let each part of your business have its time.
4. RESOLUTION. Resolve to perform what you ought; perform without fail what you resolve.
5. FRUGALITY. Make no expense but to do good to others or yourself; i.e., waste nothing.
6. INDUSTRY. Lose no time; be always employ'd in something useful; cut off all unnecessary actions.
7. SINCERITY. Use no hurtful deceit; think innocently and justly, and, if you speak, speak accordingly.
8. JUSTICE. Wrong none by doing injuries, or omitting the benefits that are your duty.
9. MODERATION. Avoid extreams; forbear resenting injuries so much as you think they deserve.

10. CLEANLINESS. Tolerate no uncleanliness in body, cloaths, or habitation.
11. TRANQUILLITY. Be not disturbed at trifles, or at accidents common or unavoidable.
12. CHASTITY. Rarely use venery but for health or offspring, never to dulness, weakness, or the injury of your own or another's peace or reputation.[7]

I think you'd agree that this is a challenging list! How did he endeavor to tackle these virtues? How would he approach the goal of perfection of character? Franklin knew that he couldn't do it all at once, so he took them one at a time: "My intention being to acquire the habitude of all these virtues, I judg'd it would be well not to distract my attention by attempting the whole at once, but to fix it on one of them at a time; and, when I should be master of that, then to proceed to another."[8] He even kept a log of his progress from day to day and week to week. He likened it to systematically weeding a garden (a metaphor that fits nicely with this book!). "And like him who, having a garden to weed, does not attempt to eradicate all the bad herbs at once, which would exceed his reach and his strength, but works on one of the beds at a time, and, having accomplish'd the first, proceeds to a second."[9]

How did he do? Well, he experienced some frustration in his efforts. "But I soon found I had undertaken a task of more difficulty than I had imagined. While my care was employ'd in guarding against one fault, I was often surprised by another."[10] He found that it was difficult to keep all of the "virtue plates" spinning at the same time without one falling to the ground, though he did see some progress. "I was surpris'd to find myself so much fuller of faults than I had imagined; but I had the satisfaction of seeing them diminish."[11]

There was another interesting development in the process. If you read the *Autobiography*, you'll notice that there are *thirteen* virtues on Franklin's list, instead of the twelve he originally developed. Where did number thirteen come from?

> My list of virtues contain'd at first but twelve; but a Quaker friend having kindly informed me that I was generally thought proud; that my pride show'd itself frequently in conversation; that I was not content with being in the right when discussing any point, but was overbearing, and rather insolent, of which he convinc'd me by mentioning several instances; I determined endeavouring to cure myself, if I could, of this vice or folly among the rest, and I added Humility to my list) giving an extensive meaning to the word.[12]

He was called out by a Quaker friend! He was blind to one of his own moral deficiencies. Here, then, is virtue number thirteen:

13. HUMILITY. Imitate Jesus and Socrates.[13]

What was his final assessment? As indicated earlier, he thought that he was better than before but never attained the perfection of virtue which he sought. It turned out that pride, identified by his Quaker friend, proved to be his undoing.

> In reality, there is, perhaps, no one of our nat-
> ural passions so hard to subdue as pride. Dis-
> guise it, struggle with it, beat it down, stifle
> it, mortify it as much as one pleases, it is still
> alive, and will every now and then peep out and
> show itself; you will see it, perhaps, often in this
> history; for, even if I could conceive that I had
> completely overcome it, I should probably be
> proud of my humility.[14]

Such is the experience of all who would try to attain moral excellence on their own. There may be temporary victories, but there will always be plates crashing to the floor. As with Dr. Franklin our own pride is at the root of the rest, the desire to do it "my way." As Solomon so profoundly expressed it three thousand years ago, "There is a way that seems right to a man, but its end is the way to death" (Proverbs 14:12).

This highlights all the more the excellence of the way that the Lord has provided for us to be in relationship with him. He sent his excellent and praiseworthy Son, who lived a morally perfect life—not even his enemies could find legitimate evidence of sin in him. He did this not with the motive of exalting himself, but to humble himself to the point of death, even death on the cross. Why? *To pay the penalty for our moral deficiencies, for our failure in every virtue.*

What an excellent and amazing plan! Peter cannot help but erupt in doxology as he considers what the Lord has done: "But you are a chosen race, a royal priesthood, a holy nation, a people for his own possession, that you may proclaim the *excellencies* of him who called you out of darkness into his marvelous light" (1 Peter 2:9, emphasis added). This is the second time Peter uses the "virtue" word, and you will notice that he uses it in plural form (*aretas*). In this verse it seems as though he is referring both to the moral excellence of God *and* to the glory of his redemptive plan. Either way, whether we are called to see the excellence of God's perfection *or* his excellent plan, he is praiseworthy.

Rather than scratching and clawing for your own status here or in the hereafter, remember that it is in the excellence of the Lord that you are secure, here and forever. Reflecting on the excellence of his glory, or on his remarkable plan, will be sure to encourage you when you're in the doldrums. When you are overwhelmed by the broken pieces of your own moral failure, remember the glory of your Savior who died for those sins and is now putting you back together piece by piece.

FROM MINDSCAPE TO LIFESCAPE: BECOMING A PERSON OF EXCELLENCE

As I try to think about a word that represents the opposite of "excellence," the word that comes to mind is "mediocrity." Here's a dictionary definition: "of only ordinary or moderate quality; neither good nor bad; barely adequate."[15] No one wants to be "barely adequate." How can you be a person of excellence? Peter provides concrete direction. Listen to this:

> His divine power has granted to us all things
> that pertain to life and godliness, through the
> knowledge of him who called us to his own
> glory and excellence, by which he has granted
> to us his precious and very great promises, so
> that through them you may become partakers
> of the divine nature, having escaped from the
> corruption that is in the world because of sinful
> desire. (2 Peter 1:3–4, emphasis added)

There are four important principles found in these verses:

1. *You have everything you need for life and godliness.* How's that for a promise? Notice that it doesn't say, "he has granted to us *some* things that pertain to life and godliness." Neither does it say, "he has granted to us *most* things that pertain to life and godliness." Rather he promises, *"all* things pertaining to life and godliness."

Sometimes we worry about our inadequacy and wonder how we can make a change in our lives or make it through the challenges we are facing. "How can we do it? The answer is that everything that we require is there for us. There is no excuse, there is no need, for failure. All things–that pertain to life and godliness have already been given us."[16] What a wonderful vista to keep in your mindscape. You have everything that you need to make it through today. God will give you direction when you are flummoxed. He will give you peace when conflict might be all around. He will give you self-control when temptation comes. When you think that the weight of grief will sink you below the waves, the buoyancy of his comfort will be there. His grace is sufficient for you for every minute of every day. Peter reminds us that this is ours "through the knowledge of him who called us." It is through the gospel of Jesus Christ that the obstacles to the true knowledge of God have been removed.

"And this is eternal life, that they know you the only true God, and Jesus Christ whom you have sent" (John 17:3). Our knowledge of God is not some abstract information but a personal relationship as his children. What's your reaction when you see your child in need? You want to meet that need in the best way that you can. In your relationship with the Father, you can know that he has promised *everything* you need for life and godliness.

2. Remember the excellence that God is determined to produce in you. Probably the most amazing phrase in this verse from Peter is the description of what God is up to in your life. He says that his plan is that "you may become partakers of the divine nature." Isn't this amazing? True moral excellence is not something that we can work up ourselves as Franklin attempted. It is the result of the Lord's excellence at work in us.

Isn't it remarkable that he speaks of becoming "partakers of the divine nature?" Why does Peter use this somewhat odd language? The same reason that Paul uses the word "virtue." He wanted to communicate with his audience. To refute his opponents he employs their terminology but gives the words a Christian meaning. Greek philosophers taught that man who is living in a corrupt world of physical pleasure must become like the gods. They advised their followers to share the divine nature. Peter resorts to using the same expression. But whereas the philosophers took their point of departure in man and claimed for him a share in the nature of the gods, Peter views our sharing of God's nature in the light of God's promises.

There is a world of difference between these two concepts. The first is humanistic and reflects the vaulted self-appraisal of natural man. The second is Christian and exalts the gracious provision of God.[17] Paul isn't saying that we become *little gods* but that we become *godly* people. We don't become identical in our being with God but rather take on the "family resemblance" as those adopted as his children in the divine plan to "be conformed to the image of his Son" (Romans 8:29). God is at work in the heart and mind of the believer. He lives within us through the presence of his Spirit.

Peter also uses the Greek word "virtue" or "excellence" to describe what flows from the life of the believer. A few verses later he writes, "For this very reason, make every effort to supplement your faith with virtue" (2 Peter 1:5). Another translation puts it this way: "in your faith supply moral excellence" (NASB). Elsewhere, Paul proclaims "I have been crucified with Christ. It is no longer I who live, but Christ who lives in me. And the life I now live in the flesh I live by faith in the Son of God, who loved me and gave himself for me" (Galatians 2:20). In union with Jesus and indwelled by the Spirit, we have everything we need for life and godliness. The challenge for us now is to be filled and empowered by the Holy Spirit. "But the fruit of the Spirit is love, joy, peace, patience, kindness, goodness, faithfulness, gentleness, self-control" (Galatians 5:22–23). There is nothing mediocre on this list. I wonder if Dr. Franklin ever came across *this* verse?

I would simply remind you that the fruit of the Spirit and excellence in character are already yours in union with Christ. Yield to the Spirit and watch them grow in your life. The Lord is not only determined to fill your *character* with excellence, but *all* that you do. Can you characterize everything you do as excellent?

Alright, I need to share one of my pet peeves, and this might upset some of my readers. I have a problem with Christian Yellow Pages. Of course I want to employ brothers and sisters in the Lord whenever I can. But you know what I've discovered? The Christian worker is not *always* the most excellent choice when it comes to getting the job done. It truly grieves me to have to say it, but I have been disappointed at times by the quality of work done by fellow Christians. Granted, this has been the exception and not the rule, but it has still surprised me when it has happened. My desire to support my brothers and sisters in the Lord must be balanced by my responsibility as a good steward of all that the Lord has given to me, which requires that I find the best quality at the best price.

As believers, we should be committed to excellence in *all* that we do so as to bring glory to our God. This means that the Christian should "serve wholeheartedly, as if you were serving the Lord, not people" (Ephesians 6:7 NIV). If you're a student, not only should your behavior in the classroom be exemplary but you should do your schoolwork as unto the Lord, doing your very best. If you're providing a service, it should be provided as requested and on time. The work of a Christian should be able to hold its own with others in a place like Angie's List, if not in fact "excel" the efforts of others. As someone once said, "It takes more time to explain why the job wasn't done right than it does to do it right in the first place!" If you do the best work that you can with the resources God has given to you, there is nothing to worry about.

3. Remember the promises. Isn't it interesting that when Peter speaks of the Scriptures in this context he refers to them as "precious and very great promises"? The means to our transformation is found in those "precious and very great promises." As we have seen in earlier chapters, the Scriptures show us his excellence and also are the means by which we are transformed. We desperately need to be reminded of what God has promised. Many volumes have been written that have sought to compile Bible promises. One of my favorites was penned by Charles Spurgeon, *The Cheque Book of the Bank of Faith.* Spurgeon's book provides one promise per day for an entire year, together with devotional thoughts. As always, there was much to be learned about the promises of God from the title itself. Here is how Spurgeon described the analogy in his introduction:

> A promise from God may very instructively be compared to a cheque payable to order. It is given to the believer with the view of bestowing upon him some good thing. It is not meant that he should have read it over comfortably, and then have done with it. No, he is to treat the promise as a reality, as a man treats a cheque.

> He is to take the promise, and endorse it with
> his own name by personally receiving it as true.
> He is by faith to *accept* it as his own. This done,
> he must believingly *present* the promise to the
> Lord, as a man presents a cheque at the counter
> of the Bank.[18]

The promises of God belong to you! Each of us has known the embarrassment of forgetting to endorse a check. We must accept each promise as a gift from God and claim it for our own.

Something else we have all experienced is carrying a check around for a long time, forgetting that we have it and failing to present it. Granted, modern technology can save us the trip to the bank counter, but we must still present the check either electronically or in person. An integral and non-negotiable factor in receiving the promised blessing is to bring it to the Lord in prayer, presenting it to him for fulfillment. "God has given no pledge which he will not redeem, and encouraged no hope which he will not fulfill."[19] We have already seen how valuable these promises are against the worry weeds that spring up in our mindscape.

Many of us have also experienced the embarrassment of a check returned for "insufficient funds." You need not worry about this as you claim the promises of God. He has even given us a promise about the promises! "For all the promises of God find their Yes in him" (2 Corinthians 1:20). This account is more than sufficient to meet the claim and to complete his commitment to develop excellence in your life.

4. Keep the past in the past. Peter also reminds us where we came from, "having escaped from the corruption that is in the world because of sinful desire." As we see the excellence of the Lord growing in your heart, don't look back. In the most vivid language, Peter declares that you have escaped bondage to sin. It indicates a decisive and permanent emancipation from that which used to enslave you. What images come to mind as you picture prisoners of war who are freed? Absolute jubilation! They would think you were crazy if you asked them if they would like to be back in bondage. Peter describes that from which we are freed as the "corruption that is in the world." The word "corruption" describes "not primarily a sudden destruction owing to external violence, but a dissolution brought on by means of internal decay, i.e., 'rottenness.'"[20] This so vividly depicts the process of decline and deterioration brought about by sin in the world and in the human soul. Peter continues to remind us that this putrefaction is fueled by "sinful desire." Human desire is not sinful in itself, but the natural desires that the Lord has given have been impacted by sin; and so, instead of meeting the natural human need for sustenance and sexual fulfillment, for example, they have become traps. These are often referred to in Scripture as sins of the flesh.

Earlier we saw Paul's list of the fruit of the life yielded to the power of the Spirit (Galatians 5:22–23). Just before these verses Paul gives another list—the list of those things to which we are most prone when operating on our own strength in our sinful nature.

> Now the works of the flesh are evident: sexual
> immorality, impurity, sensuality, idolatry, sor-
> cery, enmity, strife, jealousy, fits of anger, rival-
> ries, dissensions, divisions, envy, drunkenness,
> orgies, and things like these. I warn you, as
> I warned you before, that those who do such
> things will not inherit the kingdom of God.
> (Galatians 5:19–21)

There is nothing excellent or praiseworthy on this list! As you read it, you might see something that reminds you of the way you were. In fact, you might be reminded of a sin with which you still struggle. Remember that in Christ you have escaped the penalty of sin, you have his power at work in you to resist temptation, and one day you will be freed from the very presence of sin. So many of our worries have roots in the past.

Jesus has yanked those weeds and is about the work of making all things new.

The mediocrity and corruption of sin is no longer who you are. This process has been reversed and replaced with a process of new life in every believer. Why would you want to go back to those things that rot the soul and clutter your mindscape? Take your stand for his excellence and for his glory, remembering that he has granted you everything pertaining to life and godliness!

FOOD FOR THOUGHT

1. Why are the words "if anything is excellent or praise-worthy" an appropriate climax to Paul's description of a new mindscape?

2. What is the true standard of excellence? Where have you seen this displayed?

3. What is the difference between Ben Franklin's approach to excellence and what we've seen elsewhere in this chapter? Where are you, nonetheless, a lot more like Ben Franklin in your own approach to excellence?

4. How important are the promises of God in developing a life of excellence? Explain.

5. What are a few of your favorite "most excellent" promises from God? How can you implement them, and other of God's promises, into your life more regularly?

MEMORY VERSES

2 Peter 1:3–4: "His divine power has granted to us all things that pertain to life and godliness, through the knowledge of him who called us to his own glory and excellence, by which he has granted to us his precious and very great promises, so that through them you may become partakers of the divine nature, having escaped from the corruption that is in the world because of sinful desire."

10

Think About These Things

❧

"Worry is a thin stream of fear that trickles through the mind, which, if encouraged, will cut a channel so wide that all other thoughts will be drained out."

Author unknown

THINK ABOUT WHAT YOU THINK ABOUT

As I was planning this book I was in correspondence with Dr. David Powlison, my colleague at Westminster Seminary and the Christian Counseling and Educational Foundation (CCEF). David told me that there are three problems that "are so characteristic of human nature, and come in so many variants, that if we learn to face them in our own lives and in the lives of others, we cover the majority of ministry needs. These are always points of contact and need in every life."

What are they? Anxiety, anger, and escapism. All of them find their roots in the way we think. Anxiety is when we worry about anything and everything. Anger includes harboring bitterness, envy, and jealousy against others. Escapism "covers everything from TV obsession, immorality, overeating, etc. It reveals where people find false refuge . . . amid life's troubles and beguilements (life situation)."[1]

In our study of the scenery of the new mindscape, Paul reminds us where we can find true refuge and that we must continually "think about these things" (Philippians 4:8). The word translated "think" (*logizesthai*) means to reflect deeply or to meditate. These words do not indicate a passing thought or something to merely "keep in mind," but rather serious reflection and careful attention.

Maybe you haven't really thought much about what you think about. Hopefully, as we've walked through each of the features of a new mindscape, you've seen how important your thinking is, especially in the struggle against worry. Another way to say it is that Paul is teaching us to ground our lives in *convictions*. A conviction is a commitment we hold that influences who we are and how we live. "The principles would controul (*sic*), if the man had firm hold upon them—but his notions are superficial, his thoughts without intensity—his mind is languid and sleepy. He rather *dozes* over his principles than believes them" (emphasis original).[2] The new vistas of a new mindscape will only make a difference if we're determined to see them planted firmly in our minds rather than occasionally blowing across our thinking like tumbleweeds. This is urgent, as we have seen, because of the stubbornness of the weeds that would occupy our thoughts.

However, it is one thing to be aware of these weeds in your mindscape; it is another to actively yield to new ways of thinking.

There is no better place to conclude, therefore, than where Paul began: "whatever is true." As we saw earlier, truth is the anchor for all the rest. Are you committed to the truth *about you*? Can you handle the truth that there are weeds that desperately need attention in your mind, or are you in denial? Are you committed to the truth *about God*? Is the truth of God's revelation found in his Word foundational to your way of thinking, or is your foundation self-made? Have you admitted the reality that God is perfectly righteous and holy and not at home among the sinful weeds of your mind? Have you embraced the provision that he has made for you in his only Son who is "the way, the truth, and the life," who paid the penalty for your sins on the cross, and has now made possible a new way of thinking? It is through him that you have been promised everything you need for life and godliness. What a provision! What a promise!

I love the way Paul brings the work of Christ together with the "setting" of our hearts and minds: "If then you have been raised with Christ, seek the things that are above, where Christ is, seated at the right hand of God. Set your minds on things that are above, not on things that are on earth. For you have died, and your life is hidden with Christ in God" (Colossians 3:1–3).

We need to "reset" our thinking according to the new reality that's already ours in Christ—that, through faith in him, your salvation is already accomplished. His death is *your* death to sin; his resurrection to newness of life is *your* resurrection; and you are *already* seated with him in the heavenly places. Paul is saying: Since this is your new reality, your mindscape must expand to see everything in life from this perspective. All of the promises we've studied and all the new vistas of your new mindscape are based on this truth. We should no longer think the way we used to think.

In chapter one, you read about the Greek word for "mind" (*nous*). As we conclude, I would like to introduce you to another important Greek word: *metanoia*. The root is the word for "mind" but has a prefix that literally renders the meaning of the compound word "change of mind." The word is translated into English as "repent." The most fundamental and definitive picture of this is when we change our minds about ourselves as sufficient saviors and trust in Jesus, the One who was truly qualified to be *the* Savior. In addition to that life-transforming change of mind, we are called to an ongoing renovation of the way we think. In the very first of Martin Luther's 95 Theses he wrote, "When our Lord and Master Jesus Christ said, 'Repent' (Matthew 4:17), he willed the entire life of believers to be one of repentance."[3]

We must not allow our thoughts to be limited to ground level anymore. "Set your minds on things that are above, not on things that are on earth." We shouldn't become monks cloistered apart from the world. Rather, having our thoughts fixed on things above—on the truth about you and about the world in which we live—your perspective on who you are, what you say, and what you do will be transformed.

Don't be discouraged if this seems to be taking a long time. In fact, as Luther wrote, it takes an entire lifetime and won't be complete until we meet the Lord.

Have you realized that you're not alone in developing a new mindscape? In Christ you have been given the gift of the Holy Spirit who comes alongside you in the heavy lifting and earthmoving that will mark your life until you meet him one day. There are sinful ruts in your thinking. When you see someone better off, you envy them. When something difficult comes your way, you worry. When temptation comes your way, you yield. It's not as though you just need to move a few plants around. You need major excavation!

The Lord is determined to transform you as you meditate on whatever is "true, noble, right, pure, lovely, admirable, excellent and praiseworthy." With the Spirit's help you can excavate new paths for your thoughts. Instead of envy, you will build the path of contentment. Instead of worrying, you'll build the walk of faith. Instead of yielding to temptation, you'll find the way of escape. You cannot do it alone.

Paul's words are so urgent because these weeds and ruts are not removed once and done. Just like the battle against real weeds you must be diligent lest they come back again. This is the reason that Paul expresses himself in the present tense. You must *constantly think* about these things. There are always going to be things to worry about; therefore, you always need to remind yourself about God's faithfulness. There are always going to be others who have more than you do; there-fore, you always need to remind yourself to "seek first the kingdom of God and his righteousness, and all these things will be added to you" (Matthew 6:33). There are always going to be temptations; therefore, you must always remind yourself of the Lord's promise to provide the way of escape (see 1 Corinthians 10:13), look for it, and then take it.

The subtitle of this book is "What to Think about Instead of Worrying." I hope you can see that the reach of the new mindscape is even more extensive than countering worry. The subtitle could have been "What to Think about Instead of Worry, Envy, Jealousy, Bit-terness, Resentment, Anger, Confusion, Fear, Lust, Doubt, Sadness..." Fill in the blank with the weeds that have taken root in *your* mind. But then, meditate on "whatever is true, noble, right, pure, lovely, admirable, excellent and praiseworthy"—and you will develop new thought patterns. As you do, you'll see a new mindscape emerge, one in which the Lord is pleased to dwell.

FULL CIRCLE

Paul reminds us that this new way of thinking will trans-late into a new way of living. "What you have learned and received and heard and seen in me—practice these things" (Philippians 4:9). While he may have had more in mind, he certainly has the new vistas of verse 8 front and center. We have made the argument that a new mindscape will produce a new lifescape as well. We will not be like the Athenians who "spend their time in nothing except telling or hearing something new"

(Acts 17:21). Thinking about what you think about is not an end in itself, but an integral part of holistic transformation. As John Calvin wrote, "Now, meditation comes first, afterwards follows action."[4] What you do and what you say are reflections of what's in your heart and mind. Where there is disjunction between mind and life there is *hypocrisy*. Where there is consistency between mind and life there is *integrity*. The word "integrity" comes from a Latin root meaning "whole"—the idea being that what you see on the outside is consistent with what's on the inside. The Lord is determined to accomplish nothing less than a whole new life for you.

Paul also reminds his readers that they were not merely to remember what they "learned and received and heard" from his teaching but also *what they saw*. They were to remember what this *looked like* in Paul's life as he followed Christ. Paul practiced what he preached. Even more fundamentally, he practiced what he thought. You must remember that you are not in this alone. In the church, the Lord has given you likeminded people in whom the Lord is also doing his work. In the development of your new mindscape you need to be around others who can assist you along the way. There are lots of fellow strugglers working on their mindscapes, too.

One of the great benefits of being actively involved in a church is that you'll find people who are working on getting rid of the same weeds. When I first trusted Christ as a student in college, the Lord brought people around me who not only helped teach me about the new life but in whose lives I could see what it looked like. If you're new to the Christian faith I urge you to look for someone who can help you process the implications of Christ-centered thinking and help you with the weeds. If you've walked with the Lord for some time, find someone you can help with his or her mindscape. You'll not only be amazed at what a difference this can make in the life of the person you help, but also in yours.

"AND THE GOD OF PEACE WILL BE WITH YOU"

Earlier in our study we saw that when we pray, the peace of God will be with us. Now we come full circle as Paul promises that the "God of peace will be with you." If there is comfort knowing that there are others around to help, the ultimate consolation and encouragement is that the living God himself is with us. God has done everything in order that we might be at peace with him. Wholeness is not only a trait that should characterize our lives, but also a description of a right relationship with God. The Scriptures teach that there was once a time when we were enemies of God and antagonistic to him. However, he took the initiative to restore that relationship by sending his son to remove the obstacle to peace with God through his death on the cross. The Prince of Peace came that we might be reconciled to God. "Therefore, since we have been justified by faith, we have peace with God through our Lord Jesus Christ" (Romans 5:1).

The war is over. The alienation and divine displeasure toward us because of our sin have been removed. We are no longer objects of wrath. We have peace with God whether we realize it or not. However, to the extent that we understand and believe the truth regarding justification, we will experience a subjective peace—that is, a sense of peace within our souls. We will know that we have been brought from a state of condemnation and the prospect of eternal judgment into a state of forgiveness and favor with God.[5]

He is now *with you*. His initiative and the peace he provides is the basis of everything else. He is with you in the sense that he is *for you*.

> If God is *for us*, who can be against us? He who did not spare his own Son but gave him up *for us all*, how will he not also with him graciously give us all things? Who shall bring any charge against God's elect? It is God who justifies. Who is to condemn? Christ Jesus is the one who died—more than that, who was raised— who is at the right hand of God, who indeed is interceding *for us*. (Romans 8:31–34, emphasis added)

When you stumble and fall and relapse into old sinful ways of thinking, remember that he is "for you" in Christ. Because of his work for you, there is no basis of accusation and no possibility of ultimate condemnation—he has taken all that for you on the cross. When a child is learning to walk and stumbles and falls, his parent doesn't berate him and criticize him but rather helps him up and encourages him to try again. The parent is "for" that child. In the same way, when you stumble the Lord is eager to get you up on your feet and help you on your way, because he is "for" you.

In saying that the God of peace will be with you also teaches us of his constant *presence* with us. One of the great promises the Lord has always given his people is that he is "with" them. The greatest picture of this is the incarnation of the Son of God. The Scriptures foretold that the Messiah would be called "Immanuel," meaning "God with us." In the teaching of Jesus we hear the very truth of God, and in his life we see the character of God. Through his death, resurrection, and ascension, we have the very presence of the Lord with us through the Spirit.

> Who shall separate us from the love of Christ? Shall tribulation, or distress, or persecution, or famine, or nakedness, or danger, or sword? As it is written, "For your sake we are being killed all the day long; we are regarded as sheep to be slaughtered." No, in all these things we are more than conquerors through him who loved us. For I am sure that neither death nor life, nor angels nor rulers, nor things present nor things to come, nor powers, nor height nor depth, nor anything else in all creation, will be able to separate us from the love of God in Christ Jesus our Lord. (Romans 8:35–39)

Can anything separate you from the love of Christ? No! When you are troubled or worried or tempted to despair, remember that he is *with you* in both senses of the word: He is *for* you and he is *there for you*. Martyn Lloyd-Jones has summarized well the implications of this great truth: "Christ has blotted out our sin and therefore we can be at peace with God. And, too, he makes me at peace with myself, because as he removes sin out of my life, the stress and strain and the struggle go and I find a strange peace. He makes me live at peace with others and he enables me to be in a state of peace whatever my circumstances and conditions and surroundings might be."[6]

With these gospel assurances supporting your personal commitment, you can be sure to see progress in your mindscape as you replace worry with peace, as you replant hope in place of discouragement, and as you weed out doubts as you grow in faith in the Gardener who is determined to transform you.

FOOD FOR THOUGHT

1. How much time have you spent thinking about *what* you think about? If you were to use one word to characterize your thoughts, what would it be? To make it simpler: What has occupied your thinking today?

2. Dr. Powlison notes the big three problems (anxiety, anger, escapism) that we struggle with. Which one troubles you the most, and why? How do you see these problems work *together* against you?

3. Who have you talked to, if anyone, about the struggles you're dealing with? If you haven't spoken with anyone, who could you set aside some time to speak with (and when)? Remember, many Christians share the same challenges as you.

4. Do you really believe that God is "for you" in the struggle to change your mindscape (Romans 8:31)? How would (or does) believing it change your lifescape?

5. Of all the elements of the new mindscape (true, noble, right, pure, lovely, admirable, excellent, or praiseworthy), which have you found to be most helpful? How will you integrate each of these vistas into your mindscape going forward from here?

MEMORY VERSE

Romans 8:31–32: "If God is for us, who can be against us? He who did not spare his own Son but gave him up for us all, how will he not also with him graciously give us all things?"

Endnotes

Chapter 1: What Were You Thinking?

1. Marist Poll, "'Whatever' Still Viewed as Most Annoying Word or Phrase, Just Sayin'," http://maristpoll .marist.edu/1227-whatever-still-viewed-as-most-annoying-word-or-phrase-just-sayin (accessed 8/24/13).

2. Moises Silva, *Philippians* (Grand Rapids, MI: Baker, 2007), 197.

3. John Owen, *Spiritual-Mindedness* (Carlisle, PA: Banner of Truth, reprint 2009), 33.

Chapter 2: What? Me Worry?

1. John MacArthur, *1 and 2 Thessalonians* (Chicago: Moody, 2002), 313.

2. D. Martyn Lloyd-Jones, *The Life of Peace: An Exposition of Philippians 3 and 4* (Grand Rapids: Baker, 1992), 175.

Chapter 3: Whatever Is True

1. John Armstrong, *Feed My Sheep! A Passionate Plea for Preaching*, ed. by Don Kistler (Lake Mary, FL: Reformation Trust, 2002), 168–169.

2. "True," dictionary.com, http://dictionary.reference.com/browse/true?s=t (accessed 8/24/13).

3. The Barna Group, "Americans Are Most Likely to Base Truth on Feelings," http://www.barna.org/barna-update/article/5-barna-update/67-americans-are-most-likely-to-base-truth-on-feelings (accessed 8/24/13).

4. David Wells, *God in the Wasteland: The Reality of Truth in a World of Fading Dreams* (Grand Rapids: Eerdmans, 1994), 148–149.

5. Gordon D. Fee, *Paul's Letter to the Philippians, The New International Commentary on the New Testament* (Grand Rapids: Eerdmans, 1995), 417.

6. Armstrong, *Feed My Sheep!*, 169.

7. For more on the attributes of God, I would encourage you to take a look at *Knowing God* by J.I. Packer or if you're really feeling ambitious, *Systematic Theology* by Charles Hodge.

8. Nicki Gostin, "Morgan Freeman on why he believes he is God and which successful film he hated making," http://www.foxnews.com/entertainment/2012/07/06/fox411-qa-morgan-freeman-on-why-believes-is-god-and-which-succesful-film-hated (accessed 8/27/13).

9. "True," dictionary.com.

10. Dan Ariely, "Why We Lie," http://online.wsj.com/article/SB10001424052702304840904577422090013997320.html (accessed 8/27/13).

11. United States Secret Service, "Know Your Money," http://www.secretservice.gov/money_detect.shtml (accessed 9/30/13).

12. American Dialect Society, "Truthiness Voted 2005 Word of the Year," http://www.americandialect .org/truthiness_voted_2005_word_of_the_year (accessed 8/27/13).

13. Used by permission.

Chapter 4: Whatever Is Noble

1. Thomas à Kempis, *Of the Imitation of Christ* (Springdale, PA: Whitaker House, 1981), 43.

2. Gerald F. Hawthorne, *Philippians,* Word Biblical Commentary 43 (Nashville: Thomas Nelson, 2004), 251.

3. I-Jin Loh and Eugene Nida, *A Translator's Handbook on Paul's Letter to the Philippians* (Stuttgart: United Bible Societies, 1977), 134.

4. Fritz Rienecker and Cleon Rogers, *Linguistic Key to the Greek New Testament,* (Grand Rapids: Zondervan, 1980), 2:215.

5. "Sovereign," dictionary.com.

6. J I. Packer, *Evangelism and the Sovereignty of God* (Downers Grove: InterVarsity Press, 1961), 35–36.

Chapter 5: Whatever Is Right

1. "Moral compass," dictionary.com.

2. Bryan Nelson, "Magnetic north shifting by 40 miles a year, might signal pole reversal," http://www.mnn. com/earth-matters/climate-weather/stories/magnetic-north-shifting-by-40-miles-a-year-might-signal-pole-r (accessed 8/29/13).

3. Gordon Fee, *Paul's Letter to the Philippians,* The New International Commentary on the New Testament (Grand Rapids: Eerdmans, 1995), 417–418.

4. James Patterson and Peter Kim, *The Day America Told the Truth: What People Really Think About*

Everything that Really Matters (New York: Prentice Hall, 1991), 4.

5. Ibid.

6. Ibid., 25–26.

7. Ibid., 4.

8. Barna Group, "Americans Are Most Likely to Base Truth on Feelings."

9. Ibid.

10. John Murray, *The Imputation of Adam's Sin* (Nutley, NJ: Presbyterian and Reformed, 1977), 70.

Chapter 6: Whatever Is Pure

1. Richard Chenevix Trench, *Synonyms of the New Testament,* (Grand Rapids: Eerdmans, 1948), 333.

2. Fee, *Paul's Letter to the Philippians,* 418.

3. R.V.G. Tasker, *Matthew* (Downer's Grove: Intervarsity Press, 1983).

4. William Hendriksen, *Matthew* (Grand Rapids: Baker, 1973), 802.

5. Kaiser Family Foundation, "Sex on TV: Executive Summary 2005," http://kaiserfamilyfoundation .files.wordpress.com/2013/01/sex-on-tv-4-executive-summary.pdf (accessed 9/30/13).

6. Tom Reichert and Jacqueline Lambiase, *Sex in Advertising: Perspectives on the Erotic Appeal* (Mahwah, NJ: Lawrence Erblaum Publishers, 2003), 251.

7. "Porn Addiction Increases across the Country: Dr. Laura Bergman tells 'Live and Direct' all neighborhoods may be affected," http://www.nbcnews.com/ id/11640411/ns/msnbc-rita_cosby_specials/t/porn-addiction-increases-across-country/#.UDZL4sVO_vA (accessed 8/30/13).

8. Jonathan Edwards, "The Pure in Heart Blessed," in *The Works of Jonathan Edwards, Vol. 17: Sermons and*

Discourses 1730–1733, ed. Mark Valeri (New Haven: Yale University Press, 1999), 85.

9. C. S. Lewis, *The Screwtape Letters* (New York: Macmillan, 1943), 49.

10. Derek Thomas, Sunday evening sermon, First Presbyterian Church, Columbia, South Carolina, April 29, 2012.

11. Edwards, "The Pure in Heart Blessed," 79.

12. Ibid., 81.

13. Ibid.

14. Robert Boyd Munger, *My Heart, Christ's Home* (Downers Grove: InterVarsity Press, 1986), 3.

15. G. Walter Hansen, *The Letter to the Philippians,* The Pillar New Testament Commentary (Grand Rapids: Eerdmans, 2009), 298.

Chapter 7: Whatever Is Lovely

1. Augustine of Hippo, *Confessions,* trans. by Henry Chadwick (New York: Oxford University Press, 1992), 41.

2. Albert Mohler, "A Christian Vision of Beauty, Part One," http://www.albertmohler.com/2005/11/16/a-christian-vision-of-beauty-part-one (accessed 9/3/13).

3. Jonathan Edwards, *The Works of Jonathan Edwards, Vol. 10: Sermons and Discourses, 1720–1723,* ed. Wilson Kinnach (New Haven: Yale University Press, 1992), 421.

4. Francis Schaeffer, *Art and the Bible* (Downers Grove: InterVarsity Press, 1973), 15.

5. Sinclair B. Ferguson, "The Author of Faith," *Tabletalk,* October 2004, 29.

6. Daniel J. Wakin, "John Cage's Long Music Composition in Germany Changes a Note," *The New York Times,*

May 6, 2006, http://www.nytimes.com/2006/05/06/arts/music/06chor.html (accessed 9/3/13).

7. Francis Schaeffer, *How Should We Then Live?* (Old Tappan, NJ: F.H. Revell, 1976), 197.

8. Philip G. Ryken, *Art for God's Sake: A Call to Recover the Arts* (Phillipsburg, NJ: P&R Publishing, 2006), 42.

9. BBC News, "Sistine Chapel restored," http://news.bbc.co.uk/2/hi/europe/560315.stm (accessed 9/3/13).

10. Owen Strachan and Doug Sweeney, *Jonathan Edwards on Beauty* (Chicago: Moody, 2010), 21.

11. David Kim, The Lord Is My Shepherd (CD), http://www.cdbaby.com/cd/dkvpsjp (accessed 9/3/13).

12. Schaeffer, *Art and the Bible,* 61.

13. Ryken, *Art for God's Sake,* 41.

14. Schaeffer, *Art and the Bible,* 63.

Chapter 8: Whatever Is Admirable

1. Owen, *Spiritual-Mindedness,* 217.

2. Fee, *Paul's Letter to the Philippians,* 418.

3. Loh and Nida, *A Translator's Handbook on Paul's Letter to the Philippians,* 134.

4. Steve Artman, "Act of Sportsmanship Gives Texas High Schooler Shot at Glory," http://www.cbsnews.com/8301-18563_162-57570865/act-of-sportsmanship-gives-texas-high-schooler-shot-at-glory (accessed 9/30/13).

5. Associated Press, "Polish pilot felt huge relief after safe landing," http://usatoday30.usatoday.com/news/world/story/2011-11-02/polish-hero-pilot/51045504/1 (accessed 9/4/13).

6. Stephen Marche, "Is Facebook Making Us Lonely?" *The Atlantic,* http://www.theatlantic.com/

magazine/archive/2012/05/is-facebook-making-us-lonely/308930 (accessed 9/4/13).

7. Ibid.

8. Ibid.

9. Tim Witmer, *The Shepherd Leader at Home* (Wheaton, IL: Crossway, 2012).

10. Westminster Larger Catechism, question 148, http://www.reformed.org/documents/index.html?main frame=http://www.reformed.org/documents/larger1 .html (accessed 9/4/13).

11. Ibid., question 147.

12. David Powlison, *Seeing with New Eyes* (Phillipsburg, NJ: P&R Publishing, 2003), 114.

Chapter 9: If Anything Is Excellent or Praiseworthy

1. John Piper, *Desiring God: Meditations of a Christian Hedonist* (Colorado Springs: Multnomah, 2003), 45.

2. William Hendriksen, *Exposition of Philippians*, New Testament Commentary (Grand Rapids: Baker, 1962), 199.

3. Rienecker and Rogers, *Linguistic Key to the Greek New Testament*, 561.

4. Fee, *Paul's Letter to the Philippians*, 419.

5. Benjamin Franklin, Dixon Wecter, and Larzer Ziff, *Benjamin Franklin's Autobiography* (New York: Holt, Rinehart and Winston, 1959), 82.

6. Ibid., 83.

7. Ibid., 84–85.

8. Ibid., 85.

9. Ibid., 86.

10. Ibid., 85.

11. Ibid., 89.

12. Ibid., 93.

13. Ibid.

14. Ibid., 94.

15. "Mediocre," http://dictionary.reference.com.

16. D.M. Lloyd-Jones, *Expository Sermons on 2 Peter* (Edinburgh: Banner of Truth, 1983), 16.

17. Simon J. Kistemaker, *Exposition of the Epistles of Peter and of the Epistle of Jude* (Grand Rapids: Baker, 1987), 248.

18. Charles H. Spurgeon, *The Cheque Book of the Bank of Faith* (New York: The American Tract Society, 1893), v.

19. Ibid.

20. Rienecker and Rogers, *Linguistic Key to the Greek New Testament*, 769.

Chapter 10: Think About These Things

1. Email correspondence from David Powlison to Tim Witmer, September 20, 2006.

2. James H. Thornwell, *Discourses on Truth* (New York: Carter and Brothers, 1855), 311.

3. "Luther's 95 Theses," http://m.biblestudytools .com/history/creeds-confessions/luther-95-theses.html (accessed 10/12/13).

4. John Calvin, *Calvin's Commentaries* (Grand Rapids: Baker, repr. 1984), Vol 21, 122.

5. Jerry Bridges, *The Gospel for Real Life* (Colorado Springs: NavPress, 2003), 108.

6. Lloyd-Jones, *Expository Sermons on 2 Peter*, 201.